*"Twenty-volume folios
will never make a revolution.
It's the little pocket pamphlets
that are to be feared."*
Voltaire

IRA WELLS

On Book Banning

Or, How the New Censorship Consensus

Trivializes Art and Undermines Democracy

BIBLIOASIS
Windsor, Ontario

FIRST EDITION
10 9 8 7 6 5 4 3 2 1

Library and Archives Canada Cataloguing in Publication
Title: On book banning / Ira Wells.
Names: Wells, Ira, 1981- author
Series: Field notes (Biblioasis) ; #9.
Description: Series statement: Field notes ; 9 | Includes bibliographical references.
Identifiers: Canadiana (print) 20240522311 | Canadiana (ebook) 2024052232X | ISBN 9781771966634 (softcover) | ISBN 9781771966641 (EPUB)
Subjects: LCSH: Censorship.
Classification: LCC Z657 .W45 2025 | DDC 303.3/76—dc23

Edited by Daniel Wells
Copyedited by Chandra Wohleber
Typeset by Vanessa Stauffer
Series designed by Ingrid Paulson

Published with the generous assistance of the Canada Council for the Arts, which last year invested $153 million to bring the arts to Canadians throughout the country, and the financial support of the Government of Canada. Biblioasis also acknowledges the support of the Ontario Arts Council (OAC), an agency of the Government of Ontario, which last year funded 1,709 individual artists and 1,078 organizations in 204 communities across Ontario, for a total of $52.1 million, and the contribution of the Government of Ontario through the Ontario Book Publishing Tax Credit and Ontario Creates.

PRINTED AND BOUND IN CANADA

Contents

Who controls the past controls the future: who controls the present controls the past.

George Orwell, 1984

Introduction: The New Censorship Consensus

IN THE SPRING of 2022, the principal of my children's elementary school told a group of parents gathered to discuss a library audit that she wished she could get rid of "all the old books." The bulk of the library's holdings were, from her perspective, too Eurocentric, too male, too heteronormative. I understood these concerns, which were broadly shared among parents and teachers. Still, the prospect of liquidating several thousand library books struck me as obviously wrong—offensive not only to me personally, but also to the liberal democratic values that (however shakily) underpin our society.

I wanted to say something, but quickly checked myself: Was there not a strong chance that my opposition to removing these "harmful" books would be taken as closet racism? Or that my defense of "liberal values" in this context—a children's library, with its tiny chairs and animal posters—would come off as patently absurd? I briefly imagined how foolish I might appear—holding forth on democratic ideals like some sad imitation of Gregory Peck or Henry Fonda, everyone around me curling their toes with embarrassment.

Then the moment passed, the meeting broke up, and I was left chewing on my questions: What was so special about a bunch of old books? Were they, in fact, worth defending? Or was my fondness for these antiquated objects a product of my own nostalgia or upbringing—a sign that it was me who was antiquated?

It's true that I grew up in a bookish household, although I was not a bookish child. There were years of sports, video games, and adolescent hijinks of a tame, middle-class variety, years in which I had no career aspirations beyond making the NHL. Eventually, I found myself yearning for a more literary life, which led to the study of English. In graduate school I crossed paths with extraordinary readers—including a roommate who once read a novel while tying his shoes: He laced up one shoe, noticed a book that interested him, read it cover to cover, then laced up the other shoe and went about his day.

I read slowly by comparison, but voraciously. My job now involves teaching novels and short stories to enthusiastic university students, many of whom are budding bibliophiles; at home, I've read aloud to my own children almost every night for more than a decade and will keep doing so until the audience dries up. Many of my friendships were initiated or solidified over the giving or receiving of books, and I have now accumulated more than I might reasonably read in my lifetime. Somewhere along the way, I came to think of these objects as self-evidently valuable. I had lost (if I ever really had) the arguments to explain why books matter, and why the banning and destruction of literature is so odious and socially corrosive.

It's time to revive and sharpen those arguments. Book censorship is on the rise. We've all seen the news stories—the frequent headlines about book banning in schools or public libraries, about the takeover of school boards, about novels that are no longer teachable on university campuses, publishers pulling or issuing bowdlerized editions of suddenly controversial classics, authors who face cancellation. Not all these phenomena constitute "banning" per se, but they all fall under what we might call the new "censorship consensus," in which books are called upon to justify their existence through demonstrations of their moral value.

Many people who consider themselves book lovers seem comfortable with the new censorship consensus. Indeed, they no longer need an external authority to tell them which books ought to go. In the summer of 2024, after Andrea Robin Skinner, one of Alice Munro's daughters, came forward with the story of her harrowing sexual assault at the hands of Munro's husband (and Munro's complicity over years in covering up the abuse), readers took to X to declare that Munro had been expunged from their shelves. "I just can't . . . ," one user posted, above a photo of a garbage can filled with Munro's Nobel Prize–winning books. We've long struggled with questions about how to frame the art of people who do things we abhor, but it was the *lack* of struggle that seemed notable in this case—at least among those who had decided that Munro's work was now trash.

Books have always been challenged, but the current eruption of censorship feels like something new. "Book Bans Continue to Surge in Public Schools," went an April 2024 *New York Times* headline, which found that rates of book banning were doubling year over year.* According to PEN America, thousands of book removals occurred in 2023, in forty-two states, both Democratic and Republican. PEN has now identified more than ten thousand instances of books being removed from U.S. schools but is quick to clarify that the true number is likely much higher: One well-known study conducted by the American Library Association estimated that between 82% and 97% of all library challenges go unreported.[1] Much of this book banning appears to be fueled by outright bigotry: "Overwhelmingly, book banners continue to target stories by and about people of color and LGBTQ+ individuals," PEN notes. "30% of the unique titles banned are books about race, racism, or feature characters of color. Meanwhile, 26% of unique titles banned have LGBTQ+ characters or themes."[2]

Book bans are as old as the book itself. In my country, state-sponsored book censorship began with the passage of the Customs Act in the first session of the Canadian Parliament in 1867. That Act prohibited the importation of "books and drawings of an immoral or indecent character"; the criminal code further forbade the exhibition

....

* Similar trends have been playing out in Canada. According to a report from the organization Freedom to Read called "A Rising Tide of Censorship," Canadian libraries reported 118 "intellectual freedom challenges" in 2022–23, which represented a 50% increase from the previous year, which had itself seen a 50% increase from the year before that. These numbers, the report warned, "likely represent a very small portion of actual censorship efforts in Canadian libraries."

of any "disgusting object."[3] The United States outlawed using the Postal Service for "obscene, lewd, and lascivious" material—prohibitions backed by measures including confiscation, customs seizure, civil and criminal prosecution, and police arrests.[4]

Where book banning once largely involved the legal and disciplinary apparatus of the state, the new censorship consensus works through both state actors and a constellation of special interest groups operating inside and outside of institutions. Their target is libraries: public libraries, in which all taxpayers have a stake, and especially school libraries, which can be uniquely vulnerable due to chronic funding shortages and lack of full-time librarians able to cultivate their collections over time.

Libraries are natural quarry for anti-government organizations, including Moms for Liberty and No Left Turn in Education. Legal challenges against books, of the sort that once banned *Ulysses* and *Lady Chatterley's Lover* from American shelves, are costly and hindered by decades of First Amendment jurisprudence that steadily broadened the sphere of expressive freedom. Libraries, by contrast, are soft targets. Any citizen can mount a challenge. The instructions for doing so are often posted on the library website. Today's lawmakers are still more preoccupied with the dangers of online speech than with book bans (although that is rapidly changing in some quarters).

We should be clear on the stakes. When parental rights organizations attack libraries, they are attacking one of the last public institutions committed to intellectual freedom. While it's true that more books are now available online, we court disaster by assuming that the internet—which is volatile and ephemeral and frequently weaponized against

users across the globe—has replaced libraries as key intellectual infrastructure for liberal democracies.

Battles over book banning are especially contentious
in school libraries, for obvious reasons. We compel children to attend school, and kids *are* more impressionable,
so materials must be "age appropriate"—an inherently
debatable category. Those who would cleanse the school
library frame their efforts as an appeal to save children
from harm.

Beneath the surface of these disputes lies a deeper
conflict over our national and communal history. One
reason why book banners so frequently attack historical
fictions—including *Maus*, Art Spiegelman's graphic novel
about his father's experience as a Holocaust survivor;
Beloved and *The Bluest Eye*, Toni Morrison's haunting novels of American racial trauma, and countless other texts
at the intersection of race and history—is that the banners are fighting for control of our collective past. At the
same time, in seeking control over the narratives that
children will carry into adulthood, the banners are fighting for their vision of the future. Attacks on school libraries
are, among much else, future-oriented attacks on liberal
democracy and its vital institutions.

* * *

AMONG THE MOST influential of the U.S. parents' rights
organizations is Moms for Liberty, which the Southern
Poverty Law Center characterizes as an anti-government
extremist organization given to trafficking in conspiracy
propaganda and anti-LGBTQ+ hate.[5] The group's own membership, by contrast, understand their calls to remove

library books, including *Gender Queer* and *The Perks of Being a Wallflower*, as empowering parents and defending children from "LGBTQ indoctrination." Some of their book-banning efforts seem like social media–fuelled spectacles intended to galvanize outrage. Yet parents of a variety of religious backgrounds see their "anti-pornography" advocacy as a sincere expression of faith, and as an articulation of democratic values; their avowed aim is not to impose their beliefs upon schools or libraries, but to free children from beliefs that have been imposed upon them. Their censoriousness arises from opposition to a liberal culture that would "pollute and sexualize our children," in Florida governor Ron DeSantis's phrase.

Ontario progressives, no less than Florida conservatives, find in "child safety" a warrant to ban books. Greater sensitivity to racially charged language and imagery has resulted in school library challenges to *The Adventures of Huckleberry Finn*, *Of Mice and Men*, and several titles by Dr. Seuss. After some school districts banned from classrooms all books by non-Black authors that contain the N-word, novels like *Lord of the Flies* and *To Kill a Mockingbird* went from being mandatory to unteachable.[6]

In the fall of 2023, educators in Ontario's Peel Region (a municipality just east of Toronto, containing some 257 schools) engaged in an "equity-based book weeding process," leading some schools to purge thousands of books.[7] These books were, according to the social justice framework that motivated their removal, potential sources of student "harm."

Because no one involved with efforts to remove books from libraries characterizes their efforts as "book banning" or "censorship," some conceptual clarity is in order.

Emily Drabinski, former president of the American
Library Association, defines a book ban as "the removal
of a title from a library because someone considers it
harmful or dangerous"—which captures both equity-
based and parents' rights arguments for pulling books
from shelves. For PEN America, the definition is slightly
broader: "Any action taken against a book based on its
content that leads to a previously accessible book being
completely removed."[8] Our school principal was adamant
that she was not proposing to ban any books. Likewise,
administrators in Peel Region claim that their actions
constitute "weeding" rather than "banning," but this is a
misrepresentation of library protocol: As the American
Library Association states, "While weeding is essential to
the collection development process, it should not be used
as a deselection tool for controversial materials."[9] The
industry standard for weeding is "MUSTIE," which stands
for misleading, ugly (worn out), superseded (by a later
edition), trivial, irrelevant, and elsewhere (the item is
widely available).

These definitions do not please everyone. The American Enterprise Institute, a conservative think tank, argues
that PEN's definition of book banning is too broad,
because even if a book is banned from a school library it
may still be available from a public library or for purchase
from online vendors.[10] (A book's mere existence in
another library should console readers who lost the
opportunity to read it in theirs, and can't afford to buy it,
the AEI seems to believe.)

For others, this definition of banning (i.e., pulling
once-available books) is too narrow, as it fails to capture
books that weren't "banned" because they were never

ordered in the first place: "Progressive librarians already practice a form of book banning by not ordering books seen as 'conservative,'" argues writer and podcast host Dave Seminara.[11] Or we might be tempted to consider pre-emptive bans even further upstream in the publishing process.[12] "Random House Canada staff try to ban Jordan Peterson's new book," the *Daily Mail* declared in a headline, after the firm received seventy anonymous complaints about publishing *Beyond Order: 12 More Rules for Life*.[13] By this logic, Woody Allen's memoir was "banned" by Hachette, the publisher who cancelled it, and then "unbanned" by Arcade Publishing, who printed 75,000 copies. And the decision of Tundra Book Group (which includes Penguin Teen Canada and Puffin Canada) to limit their submission policy exclusively to LGBTQIA2S+, BIPOC, disabled, and refugee writers constitutes a de facto pre-publication ban on books by everyone else.[14] Such questions lead us down a rabbit hole of metaphysical considerations around when a book becomes a book, or whether you can ban the "idea" for a book that does not exist.

The truth is that publishers have always shaped their lists according to their editorial priorities and business practices, just as individual booksellers stock only a tiny fraction of the millions of titles available at any given moment; neither should be conflated with book banning. Similarly, conflicts between the ideals and business imperatives of publishers (and between their employees and paying readership) lie beyond our scope (which is not to say that an illiberal culture of policing and regulating what gets produced, and by whom, is not worthy of consideration). But even former ALA president Emily

Drabinski's relatively narrow definition of book ban ("the removal of a title from a library because someone considers it harmful or dangerous") leaves an alarming number and range of incidents to consider.[15]

* * *

IN RESEARCHING HOW books are removed from library shelves, I wanted to learn more about how they end up on those shelves in the first place. Lisa Radha Vohra, Director of Collections and Membership Services at the Toronto Public Library (TPL), which consists of over a hundred branches, explained that the acquisitions process for most North American libraries begins with material selection policies. Those policies are "grounded in the broadest definition of intellectual freedom," Vohra says, "meaning that public libraries intentionally work to have balanced collections, and acknowledge that some materials in collections will be offensive to some people." Most public libraries endorse the American Library Association's definition of intellectual freedom as "the right of every individual to both seek and receive information from all points of view without restriction."[16]

The selection policies lay the groundwork for acquisitions across a broad array of categories, including materials which educate, entertain, provide aesthetic experiences and stimulate creativity, and provide varying viewpoints on current and historical issues and controversies. Policies for challenging and "de-accessioning" books are similarly grounded in the principle of intellectual freedom. Material may "be considered offensive by Library customers," but the library "does not accord to any individual or group the right to restrict the freedom of others to make use of that same material."[17]

Vohra acknowledges that those involved in selection processes are human beings with their own preferences and biases. One way of correcting for those biases includes robust policy language (which commits, in TPL's case, to providing "the widest possible range of resources"). Another is including people of different backgrounds and perspectives on selection committees.

"There is never one person responsible for the selection of materials," Vohra told me. "Ideally, the group of five or six individuals doing adult fiction selection are able to balance each other's life experiences, biases, knowledge, reading habits, and so on." Like most public libraries, TPL also has a "recommend a title" feature, in which members of the public can request material they can't find. During the pandemic, customers pointed out that TPL hadn't acquired Robert F. Kennedy Jr.'s *The Real Anthony Fauci*, in which Kennedy accused the U.S.'s top infectious-disease doctor of funding "rigged scientific research" and pursuing "truly a dark agenda." The TPL currently has twelve copies, with seventeen holds.

The TPL is a large, comparatively well-resourced institution. Still, according to Vohra, the vast majority of North American libraries—she estimates 90–95%—follow similar processes when it comes to acquiring books. These institutions are more motivated by customer demand than by enforcing ideological conformity. "If there's demand, we're going to get it," Vohra says. "If the system shows that the Trump books are moving, we'll get more Trump books."

School libraries are different. Their selection procedures are usually informed by board-level policies and other jurisdictional laws and regulations. School libraries are narrower in scope than public libraries, and geared more toward education than entertainment. While nominally expected to uphold intellectual freedom and to nurture a love of reading, school libraries exist mostly to support the curriculum.[18] Within the curricular context, "resources may represent different perspectives," writes Anita Brooks Kirkland, chair of Canadian School Libraries. "But," she adds, "it is very important to understand that that does not mean that all points of view should be represented." Students interested in "differing viewpoints for controversial topics" are invited to explore a research database called Opposing Viewpoints, which links to "professionally-selected resources."[19]* This database, Kirkland seems to believe, is the counterweight necessary to achieve what she calls a "balanced" library.

* * *

WHEN CONSIDERING THE origins of contemporary book banning, we can point to material causes: We can follow, for example, the hundreds of thousands of dollars that Patriot Mobile, a self-identified Christian cellphone carrier, devoted to promoting Texas school board candidates who were committed to eliminating critical race theory and "LGBTQ indoctrination" from schools.[20] We can point to political causes: Texas governor Greg Abbott's 2021 campaign promise to investigate a list of about 850 books that might cause students "psychological distress because

....

* For what it's worth, my own middle and high school–aged children, both of whom attend Ontario public schools, had never heard of Opposing Viewpoints.

of their race or sex," or legislative efforts in Florida, Utah, and Missouri aimed at removing LGBTQ content from school libraries. We can examine a British Columbia school board's decision to pull *The Absolutely True Diary of a Part-Time Indian* by Sherman Alexie, *In the Heat of the Night* by John Ball, and *To Kill a Mockingbird* by Harper Lee from a grade ten reading curriculum over student safety concerns.[21] But all of this unfolds against a broader context in which the cultural value of books and reading seems to be waning.

The rise of contemporary book banning presents a paradox. Book banners assign extraordinary power to books at a time when, by objective measures, books and literature seem to matter less and less. One survey found that about half of Americans didn't read a single book in 2023.[22] English departments have seen declining enrollments for a generation; increasingly, students arrive at university having never read an entire book in high school.[23] In classrooms across North America, teachers are assigning ever-fewer full-length books; instead, they provide summaries and key passages.

This turn away from books ("paywalled dead trees," as the tech bros call them[24]) is becoming educational policy. In 2022, the U.S. National Council of Teachers of English released a clear position statement on media literacy: "The time has come to decenter book reading and essay-writing as the pinnacles of English language arts education."[25] Students, too, seem glad to be rid of books: According to the U.S. Bureau of Labor Statistics, Americans between fifteen and nineteen read for personal interest for an average of eight minutes per day; no age group reads less.[26] This, at a time when teens are spending a median of almost four and a half hours daily on their smartphones.[27] The typical teen spends more time on their phone each day than they spend reading over an entire month.

At a historical moment in which social media and digital technology occupy an increasingly central role in children's lives, it seems strangely nostalgic to fret about the power of books to, for example, "indoctrinate" children into adopting a queer lifestyle, or, for that matter, to psychologically harm them with non-inclusive narratives. You might think, in short, that parents concerned with saving children from the baleful effects of media would focus their attention upon the forms of media that their children actually consume.*

But that is to presume that book banning is expected to work, and it rarely has. At least, not if we believe that the work of book banning is to eliminate dangerous or harmful or otherwise subversive ideas, however those ideas are defined. Two thousand years ago, for reasons that remain murky, the Roman Senate decreed that the books of historian Aulus Cremutius Cordus were to be burned. As the Roman historian Tacitus would later record in his *Annals*,

> The Fathers ordered his books to be burned ... but some copies survived, hidden at the time, but afterwards published. Laughable, indeed, are the delusions of those who fancy that by the exercise of

....

* Towards that end, in 2024 eight Ontario school boards and two private schools launched lawsuits, seeking over $7 billion in damages, against social media companies (including the owners of Facebook, Instagram, Snapchat, and TikTok) for marketing intentionally addictive products to children and for "rewiring" the way children "think, act, behave and learn."

ephemeral power, posterity can be defrauded of information. On the contrary, through persecution, the reputation of the persecuted talent grows stronger. Foreign despots and all those who have used the same barbarous methods have only succeeded in bringing disgrace upon themselves and glory to their victims.[28]

As Tacitus recognized, book bans can achieve the opposite of their desired effect, increasing people's desire to read what authorities would prohibit. "Every time a school district bans *Thug*, the sales in that area skyrocket," tweeted *The Hate U Give* author Angie Thomas. Direct action against authors can bring similar results. On Friday, August 12, 2022, Salman Rushdie's novels weren't charting on the Amazon top 100 bestsellers. Then he was stabbed. By the following Tuesday, *The Satanic Verses*— the "blasphemous" novel that had prompted Ayatollah Ruhollah Khomeini to issue the fatwa ordering Rushdie's execution in 1989—had topped several of Amazon's bestseller lists.[29]

Yet there's no denying that censorship has wrought devastating effects. Writing by Ovid, Confucius, Mikhail Lermontov, and countless others may have been censored out of existence; great libraries have been reduced to rubble; writers have been tortured and burned. Missionaries including Diego de Landa destroyed Mayan codices and Inca quipus, part of what is now understood as a broader genocidal campaign aimed at eliminating all cultural traces of pre-Christian North America.[30] Untold monuments to human culture have been permanently lost; many more have failed to materialize under authoritarian regimes in which expressive freedom must fly under the radar of secret police. If calls to censor Angie Thomas and Salman Rushdie lead to increased sales in the Anglosphere, that is because a robust culture of expressive freedom continues to allow for the celebration of challenged books. And it is precisely this culture of expressive freedom that today's book banners erode by normalizing censorship.

Still, given the ubiquity of digital technology that allows for near-instantaneous reproduction of material, the complete eradication of texts may strike us as increasingly implausible. Never has it been easier to upload, disseminate, or find challenged books on the internet (at least theoretically—library patrons without the technology, time, or money to source the book elsewhere will disproportionately suffer the effects of book bans). The prospect of eliminating a book's existence, or preventing determined readers from accessing it, has never been more fanciful than for contemporary North Americans.

Which brings us to a second paradox of contemporary censorship: In an era where book banning feels less feasible than ever, more and more people are attempting it, which forces us to think again about their goals. The new censorship consensus does not "work" as censorship once did, through pre-publication licences or the efforts of customs officers charged with confiscating and destroying contraband literature.

Instead, it works as symbolic practice, as means for the book banners to announce what they would extirpate from the library, and not only from the library. Book banning may be a symptom of political impotence, in the sense that it does nothing to alleviate underlying conditions: Peel Region is no less racist for having expunged thousands of pre-2008 library books, and the racialized student who came to school without breakfast before the book purge is still coming to school without breakfast.[31] Banning *All Boys Aren't Blue* from the library won't prevent children's acquaintance with LGBTQ+ ideas, nor will it hasten the dawn of a new golden era of traditional gender roles in American society.

But it may work in other ways, and the "success" of book banning needn't be understood as zero-sum. Today's book banners may care less about permanently eradicating certain books or ideas than about temporarily limiting access during an impressionable life stage. The effect may be to deprive a queer student of the solace of literary representation at a moment when it was needed most. Regardless of the final availability (or not) of any challenged book, book banning may perform the political work of uniting community members against a perceived threat, of defining group affiliation through opposition to an imagined Other. It constitutes a form of symbolic violence, where purged books represent what banners would purge from society itself—and where the act of purging constitutes a rite of belonging.

The parental rights movement's calls to resist "pornography" and "LGBTQ indoctrination" now enjoys significant political support. When he was running for re-election, Donald Trump inveighed against school board "dictatorships" at the 2024 Moms for Liberty Summit. "Your schools and your children are suffering greatly because they're going into the classrooms and taking disease," he warned.[32] For years, state legislatures have been passing bills that would prohibit teaching sexual or racial concepts in schools. Some of these have been struck down as unconstitutional, and more will be. Regardless, the fate of *Roe v. Wade* serves as a reminder that legal freedoms remain fragile; the return of regressive censorship committees, postal searches, and prosecutions remains a live possibility. Those in favour of such a regime can find inspiration not only in our own recent history, but also in the systems of censorship currently thriving in authoritarian regimes around the world.

For now, we fight about schools, about what the children, who read less and less, should read. Contemporary progressive educators from Ontario bear little in common with parents' rights activists from Florida, and their aims are not equivalent. But both treat books as sources of contagion and libraries as fields of indoctrination, and both invoke the vulnerability of children as a warrant for censorship. Both abide by the new censorship consensus, where the school library is a microcosm of the ideal society, and books are levers of social engineering. *In my ideal society*, their thinking goes, *there will be more of this, and less of that: more diversity, less racism.* Or: *More Socrates and Shakespeare, less wokeness.* Both ignore the cyclical nature of censorship, presuming that the new censorship apparatus won't eventually come for them. They deceive themselves.

* * *

OVER THE PERIOD in which I was writing this book, people would often ask me about the "cause" of book banning. The truth is that there is not one cause but many, and these causes are entwined with many of the social, political, and economic upheavals that have shaped the last several decades. They include the widespread erosion of public trust in expertise and public institutions of all kinds—a phenomenon driven by failures of technocratic experts that are both real (forever wars, trade policies that ravaged manufacturing communities, and super-charged income inequality) and imagined (in the form of viral conspiracy theories featuring bloodsucking reptilian humanoids). Further causes include the tribalization of political identity and arrival of social media algorithms that exacerbate those divisions. They include the mani-fest failure of liberal-democratic societies to live up to self-proclaimed ideals of equality—failures which begat political movements (such as Black Lives Matter and LGBTQ+ campaigns), and which inflame conservative counter-reactions (MAGA and its offshoots, including parental rights advocacy groups).

Some of these broad social trends contribute to book bans indirectly, engendering a sense that those in charge of institutions cannot be trusted, or creating conditions of economic precarity in which citizens, feeling out of control, look for things they *can* control: You can't purge TikTok of LGBTQ+ content, but maybe you can pull a few books from library shelves. Sometimes, however, the link between larger social forces and book banning is more direct: In Ontario's Peel Region, for instance, high immi-gration levels resulted in a large demographic change over a short time; diverse student bodies were left with library books that suddenly felt unrepresentative. The cause of this asymmetry was not racism but relatively welcoming immigration policies. Yet the 2020 police kill-ing of George Floyd confirmed for many progressives around the world that racism was the transhistorical driver of social inequality. In this context, the old liberal pieties, the Constitution's "self-evident truths," struck activists as dangerous anachronisms conceived by slave-holding aristocrats. Appeals to "free speech" carried a whiff of revanchism, as though they necessarily entailed a defense of the racist status quo.

Meanwhile, the tone of public discourse, which had been intensifying for decades, seemed to reach a new, frantic crescendo. The signature rhetorical tic was "now, more than ever." Every election was the most important of our lifetimes. We took the weightiest words in our language, words like "existential" and "Nazi," and tossed them around like rhetorical confetti. An insensitive word can now undermine someone's very right to exist. Life became one long linguistic emergency, a state of exception requiring an exceptional response.

If the social media pressure cooker was part of the problem, it also presented a solution: the "block" button, which ensured that every user could be her own censor. Back in 2014, the activist Suey Park encountered a post from the official Twitter account of *The Colbert Report*. Park found the post to be racially derogatory toward Asians, and replied with a hashtag: #CancelColbert— inaugurating a new "culture" of cancellation which came for legions of users (Park included), even as others insisted that "cancel culture" did not exist. All the while, the *medium* of social media, its interfaces and ubiquitous vocabulary of cancellation, acclimatized users to a culture of censoriousness.[33]

Our literary culture was rewiring itself around a more stringent set of norms, and some could or would not keep up. In 2018, Ian Buruma, editor of the *New York Review of*

Books, published an essay by the disgraced Canadian broadcaster Jian Ghomeshi, who had been acquitted in 2016 of choking and sexual assault charges. When the piece ignited a maelstrom of controversy, Buruma tried an old argument, encouraging readers to separate the tale from the teller. The story, from the "point of view of somebody who has been pilloried in public opinion," was of legitimate interest in itself, he argued in a *Slate* interview; as for Ghomeshi's sexual behavior, or "how much consent was involved—I have no idea, nor is it really my concern," Buruma said.[34] Five days after the Ghomeshi story was published, Buruma was no longer editor of the magazine.[35]

Buruma's ouster was part of a larger shift in public attitudes around the moral purpose of art and literature. Critical reception of all manner of cultural products, from novels to Broadway musicals to Disney movies, increasingly hinged upon their political dimensions. Those dimensions had always been there, of course, and feminist and Marxist critics had long argued for art's irreducibly political nature: as Carol Hanisch insisted in the title of a 1969 essay, "The Personal Is Political," while Pierre Bourdieu famously argued in 1979's *Distinction* that the very purpose of art was "to fulfill a social function of legitimating social differences," by which he meant that art always naturalized social hierarchies. Now, after a decade defined by #MeToo (which made it difficult to detach art from the heinous moral transgressions of its creator); #OscarSoWhite and related campaigns (which focused our attention squarely upon injustices in racial representation); and various "Pretendian" controversies (including those around Buffy Sainte-Marie and the writer

Joseph Boyden, which had further reinforced the link between art and identity), the political implications of art assumed centre stage.

The tenor of the conversation about the arts reflected this, especially in legacy media institutions like the Canadian Broadcasting Corporation and the *New York Times*. Insofar as arts coverage had ever concerned itself with the aesthetic or formal properties of the work, with its techniques and themes and meaning, those considerations were now superseded by a new vision of art's purpose, one summarized by Simon Brault, chief executive of the Canada Council for the Arts (Canada's federal funder): "We need to reimagine an arts sector determined to eliminate racism and discrimination in every form, and the legacy of colonialism. We need to reimagine the arts' rightful place in the conversations that shape our future."[36] These priorities, baked into the funding criteria of granting agencies, animated arts criticism that celebrated diversity or questioned whether a writer like Jeanine Cummins was "allowed" to write *American Dirt*, or whether Quentin Tarantino's profligacy with the N-word had put him beyond the pale. Cultural organizations further solidified the link between art and politics by publishing solidarity statements after (select) national and global calamities.

Let me be clear. The politicization of art over this period was the product of real, intractable problems, and the calling out of these problems—systemic racism, sexism, cultural genocide, environmental despoliation—is essential to the promise of perfectibility that underlies the legitimacy of liberal democracies. Next to the enormity of these problems, art's "aesthetic" concerns came to be viewed as trivial. If literature had once publicly aspired to beauty, truth, surrealism and absurdity, divinity, pleasure, or basic entertainment, the urgency of our causes exposed those considerations as privileged. Political questions (whether a book was, in Simon Brault's words, committed to "eliminating racism and discrimination in every form") supplanted aesthetic ones (such as whether that text resisted formal conventions or recycled clichés). Where critics had once seen their work in terms of taking the implicit assumptions of a text and making them explicit (or, in Fredric Jameson's terms, exposing art's "political unconscious"), in our era of consciousness-raising, the critic's role was to praise or call out what was already on the surface. Artists turned away from aesthetic mediation, embracing autofiction, direct-to-camera monologues in TV shows and Instagram reels, immersive art exhibits, and first-person memoir.[37] The sought-after effects are immediacy, realness, a collapsing of the distinctions between the artist and art, and an appeal to the real-world utility of social justice.

There were exceptions, of course—artists and critics who rejected the overt politicization of their work, but they were increasingly peripheral to the institutional mainstream.* And once we had agreed that art was politics, we could get down to the business of sorting. Educators devised literal checklists and rubrics to help school librarians make judgments about which "resources" should

---

* Consider critic James Wood. Two decades ago, Wood's aesthetic interventions (such as "hysterical realism," a term he invented to describe the manic storytelling of Salman Rushdie, David Foster Wallace, Zadie Smith, and others) sparked attention and debate. His criticism has, to my mind, grown finer with the passage of years, and yet I can't remember the last time a piece of Wood's criticism attained anything resembling virality. Our algorithms do not share Wood's aesthetic concerns.

arm the shelves; the rest of us carried our invisible rubrics around in our heads, while our participation in the online world was mediated by algorithms we neither saw nor understood.

* * *

ONE FINAL FACTOR is necessary for book banning to take off. And that is the erosion of intellectual freedom as a public value. Over the last fifteen years, arguments for intellectual freedom and free speech have come to be regarded as philosophically naïve or as a smokescreen for right-wing hate.

There are obvious and less obvious reasons for this. In its 2010 *Citizens United* decision, the U.S. Supreme Court lifted century-old campaign finance restrictions, allowing corporations and wealthy donors to contribute unlimited sums to political campaigns. Why? Because, in the view of the court's majority, the old campaign finance limits amounted to a suppression of political speech. But if money *is* speech, then speech is subject to the same inequalities endemic to neoliberal financial markets. Sure, every citizen is nominally "free" to speak her mind on social media, but everyone knows that those with deeper pockets, legacy media connections, and round-the-clock public relations teams have "freer" speech than the rest of us, because they command attention.

Meanwhile, the "free speech" mantle was taken up by far-right internet provocateurs, including (to cite just one) Milo Yiannopoulos, who, in 2016–17 engaged in his "Dangerous Faggot" tour of college campuses, in which he ridiculed minorities and proclaimed that "feminism is cancer."[38] Many progressives took one look at these developments and concluded that "free speech" had become a dog whistle for demagoguery. "The defense of free speech promises to restore a traditional cultural order," William Davies argued in a 2018 *Guardian* article titled "The free speech panic: how the right concocted a crisis." The very idea of free speech, Davies insisted, was "a romantic ideal extracted from the past," taken up in service of unfettered capitalism, xenophobia, and bigotry.[39]

Many disagreed with this analysis and openly criticized what they saw as a new culture of censoriousness. In 2020, 152 writers, including Margaret Atwood, Noam Chomsky, and Cornel West, signed "A Letter on Justice and Open Debate" in *Harper's*, which spoke of "a new set of moral attitudes and political commitments that tend to weaken our norms of open debate and toleration of differences in favor of ideological conformity."[40] In response, 160 less well-known writers and academics signed "A More Specific Letter on Justice and Open Debate," which portrayed the *Harper's* letter as reactionary backlash, in which a threatened elite demonstrated "an unwillingness to dismantle systems that keep people like them in and the rest of us out." The *Harper's* letter, they argued, had missed the fundamental point: that "marginalized voices have been silenced for generations in journalism, academia, and publishing."[41]

These arguments found support in the work of academics who, for decades, had been raising questions about "free speech" as an unexamined value. Many scholars of queer and racialized histories argued—correctly—that the freedoms afforded by the First Amendment had always been unevenly distributed: If there was some liberal "golden age" of free expression, it had never included, say, queer presses and bookstores, which were persecuted well into the 1980s and 1990s. Other scholars, following in the footsteps of Michel Foucault, went further, arguing that it was wrong to think of censorship as "repressive," and that censorship was more accurately understood as "productive" and "generative" of speech itself. English professor Stanley Fish captured the zeitgeist in the title of his 1994 book, *There's No Such Thing as Free Speech ...And It's a Good Thing, Too*.

These arguments offer sobering diagnoses of the ways in which nation-states and institutions have failed to live up to the universal promise of their own ideals. Free speech has never existed in a perfect regime of rights that applies equally and democratically to all citizens; nor does free speech absolutism exist as a coherent philosophical concept, as anyone opposed to the teaching of creationism or Holocaust denialism in schools has already conceded.

But this doesn't mean that expressive freedom cannot be *further* curtailed. History reveals the endless ways in which it is possible to become *less* free. Free speech may not exist, but we'll miss it when it's gone.[42] The fact that we cannot yet point to a place or time in which the ideal of free speech has taken worldly form does not mean that we should abandon it as an ideal, or that we should cede ground to those who would circumscribe our fragile, imperfect freedoms. Censorship, by its very nature, seeks to limit the scope of the imaginable: We resist it by rededicating ourselves to imaginative commitments, not least freedom of speech.

Book banning thrives in an intellectual culture in which art is not analyzed for its inevitable political assumptions but reduced to them, in which books and reading are devalued, and in which anti-censorship arguments are tainted as reactionary. It also thrives when people fail to articulate why reading imaginative literature matters—when they find themselves, as I did, unable to succinctly describe in an elementary school library why it's wrong to throw out every "old" book.

It's one thing to defend reading on the grounds of "access to information," as librarians often do, or as sheer entertainment, a means of passing time on the beach. But it's harder to explain why reading imaginative literature matters. We turn to authorities like Ursula K. Le Guin, who argues that literature "is one of the most useful tools we have for achieving meaning: it serves to keep our communities together by asking and saying *who we are*, and it's one of the best tools an individual has to find out *who I am*." C. S. Lewis argues that, as humans, we yearn to "see with other eyes, to imagine with other imaginations, to feel with other hearts, as well as with our own," and that only literature affords this "enlargement of our being." For Allan Bloom, the most important books "bring us light from outside our cave, without which we would be blind."[43]

I find these (and many other) defences of literature both stirring and strangely dissatisfying. They never quite capture the entire experience of reading a novel by Ralph Ellison or Jane Austen, Yaa Gyasi or Miriam Toews. The best novels are never reducible to a "message," political or otherwise.[44] They are internally conflicted, containing multiple voices and viewpoints, arguments and counter-arguments, conflicting messages, a surplus that exceeds the author's own design. There is a reason for the eternal popularity of book clubs: because literature nudges us toward conversation, unsettles us with questions, and leaves us suspended in indeterminacy. The best books demand further discussion, on Goodreads or BookTok or YouTube or the books section of a newspaper, in stage or screen adaptations, in fan fiction, or only within ourselves.

Censorship confronts us with literature's opposite. Where literature opens conversations, censorship closes them. Where literature provokes questions, censorship insists upon answers. Where literature unsettles us with ambiguity, the realization that the "meaning" of a text is never final, censorship seeks to comfort us with moral absolutes.

Throughout history, book banners have sought to deprive readers of specific information, which is anti-democratic. But they would also restrict your personal choices about what to read, which is illiberal. If being a citizen in a liberal democracy means anything, it entails autonomy of mind: We are free to choose how to educate ourselves, how to think and what to think about, and what to read. These choices are profoundly personal. Our reading reflects the quality of consciousness we hope to cultivate, the nature of wisdom to which we aspire, the mental lives we choose to lead. This is what makes book banning so deeply offensive: It represents an attack on your intellectual autonomy, your right to determine the future of your own mind. It would prevent you from becoming the person you want to be.

All of this and more I had hoped to communicate to the school principal who wanted to purge the old books. When you trash, ban, or otherwise censor library books, you desecrate the principle that a free people must be free to develop their own minds. When you teach a child that censorship is the correct response to uncomfortable ideas, you pander to the student and contribute to the erosion of democracy itself. And when you trash books, it is not only those specific volumes that are gone; you also carry out a symbolic attack on knowledge, culture, continuity, and community.

In the end, I did not try to condense these arguments into an impromptu speech for the benefit of the principal and small group of parents. It is perhaps just as well that my response to those who would liquidate books comes in the form of the modest volume now cradled in your hands. Just what the world needs: a new book.

1. Banning Books to Save Children

IN APRIL 2022, a routine administrative update from my children's public elementary school called for parental involvement in an upcoming "library audit." I wondered what was behind this exercise and was later informed that the audit's goals included "creating a culture of student well-being" and "transforming student learning for success," which didn't exactly clarify things. I worried we were seeing the beginnings of a book banning process, the likes of which had been turning school libraries into acrimonious ideological battlegrounds across the United States.

PEN, the free speech organization, had already sounded the alarm. Their 2022 report *Banned in the USA* cited 2,532 instances of individual books being banned, impacting 1,648 distinct titles. Often, this involved concerted state efforts or educational gag orders, such as Florida's Parental Rights in Education Act—the so-called "Don't Say Gay" law—which pressured schools to pull LGBTQ+ content from their shelves. While Canadian schools had mostly avoided rancorous debates over book censorship, our children's principal now appeared to be wading in, albeit from the opposite side.

The books most subject to banning in the U.S.—Maia Kobabe's *Gender Queer*, Angie Thomas's *The Hate U Give* (informed by the Black Lives Matter movement), and Raina Telgemeier's LGBTQ+ friendly graphic novel *Drama*, among them—receive pride of place in Toronto school libraries, displayed face-forward like the best-sellers at Indigo or Barnes & Noble. What concerned our principal were books from a previous era, which may be read to reaffirm heteronormative, patriarchal, or Euro-centric cultural norms.

Our school had already placed equity—an umbrella term for anti-racism, anti-oppression, gender inclusivity, and Indigenous advocacy—at the heart of its work. In a message to parents, the principal promised to bring an "equity perspective" to "all major decision-making discussions, including school budget, school council supports, program or service priorities, and human and non-human resources."

My question was what the equity perspective would have to say about *Charlotte's Web*, *Where the Wild Things Are*, or *Bridge to Terabithia*. Would such books withstand scrutiny from an anti-oppression standpoint, or were they to be written off as products of a less enlightened age? What would happen if they were?

When I asked administrators about the exercise, the principal assured me the aim was not to ban books. "This action is meant more to be a reflection tool and prompts for ongoing discussion," she wrote, "rather than removing texts from the shelves, unless the resources are explicitly harmful in their representation of groups of peoples." But who, I wondered, would judge whether books were explicitly harmful? (What about books that were merely *implicitly* harmful?) What criteria would be used to measure the harm, and how would they be applied? The only way to find out, I decided, was to join the committee.

So, one sunny morning in late May, armed with my Toronto District School Board Equity Toolkit, a checklist to guide our work, I joined a handful of self-conscious parents outside our school library. Before long, we were pulling books from the shelves for inspection, and I was writing myself into a history of censorship that is as old as literacy itself.

* * *

One of the epicentres of contemporary book banning is Escambia County, Florida, on the westernmost edge of the Panhandle. Some historians contend that Pensacola, the county seat, saw the first shots of the American Civil War. In February 2023, another conflict was brewing in Pensacola, as parents and community members gathered for a special school board meeting devoted to "reconsideration of educational materials." The agenda included votes on three books that were subject to "citizen challenge": *All Boys Aren't Blue*, the memoir of a Black LGBTQ activist, *When Aidan Became a Brother*, about a trans boy, and *And Tango Makes Three*, an illustrated book about two male penguins who raise a baby penguin in the Central Park Zoo. These were among more than one hundred titles that had been challenged by a single district high school teacher, Vicki Baggett. A state-mandated Instructional Materials Review Committee, consisting of parents, teachers, and administrators, had already determined that all three books had educational merit and that Baggett's complaint was unfounded. The board, however, would have the final say, and the mood was tense.

Decisions would be made on a book-by-book basis, and members of the public used their allotted speaking time to debate whether the books were "age-appropriate, agenda-setting, or a flat-out abomination before God," according to the Pensacola News Journal. Many justified their opposition with appeals to a higher power: God "gave marriage as a beautiful picture of his relationship with His people. But we want to distort that picture, because we hate God," argued Joshua Luther, a community member who believed it was un-Christian to normalize same-sex marriage, even in a parable about penguins. "All the people that come to defend these books need to repent," Luther declared.

Rick Branch, a minister at the local First United Methodist Church, disagreed, arguing that Jesus would have wanted his followers to build inclusive spaces. "I have seen the hurt that has been caused by people who say God doesn't love you the way you are," said the minister. "I am a white, Anglo-Saxon, cisgender, Protestant, Christian male. I can find myself reflected in society anywhere. But for this book [All Boys Aren't Blue]—Black, queer, youth— they can't find that everywhere."

The debate ground on for nearly five hours. In the end, it wasn't even close. The board voted 5–0 to overturn the review committee's earlier decision, deeming the books unsuitable even for optional reading and subject to immediate removal. "I believe in parental rights," explained one board member, emphasizing that parents could buy their children any books they pleased, but that *these* books—one of which pushed an "LGBTQ agenda using penguins"—had no place in Escambia school libraries.[45]

One student in attendance, Ella Jane Hoffmaster, had a different takeaway. "I am currently embarrassed to be a student in Escambia County tonight," she said.[46]

Unfortunately for Hoffmaster and other students, the book banners of Escambia County were just getting started. A meeting about the next challenged book, *Ground Zero*—Alan Gratz's novel about the historical impact of September 11, 2001, told through the eyes of American and Afghan children—was just a couple of days away.

* * *

THE MEETINGS DEVOTED to challenged books continued throughout that spring, with tensions escalating on both sides. Concerned citizens met up in parking lots to distribute matching T-shirts and divvy up their talking points. More than 150 people, including children, turned up to debate *Drama* by Raina Telgemeier, *The Bluest Eye* by Toni Morrison, *The Nowhere Girls* by Amy Reed, and *New Kid* by Jerry Craft. These challenges, too, had come from Vicki Baggett, who cited "indoctrination of LGBTQ," "sexual introductions," "race-baiting," and "anti-whiteness."[47]

"My [classroom] space will always be a safe place for trans kids, Black kids, and any other kid who needs a safe space," said West Florida High School social studies teacher Jerrod Novotny. "Majority rule does not make minorities' rights obsolete ... Diverse stories are essential [because] they validate the experience of those who can see themselves."

The pro-censorship contingent doubled and tripled down on their religious convictions. "The Bible says that these things [homosexual relationships] are unnatural," said Aaron Schneier, a local handyman who had become a fixture at the board's meetings. "We don't need to bring perverted things and perversion for our children. There is a day of judgment coming and I wish that you all would know—it's not funny—the blood of Jesus Christ."[48]

On this occasion, after nearly eight hours of debate, the board sided with the books, deciding that all four could remain on the shelves. Some grumbled about the board being "inconsistent."

"There was an incredible amount of pressure from the community on the school board members as they made their decisions," Brittany Misencik, a reporter who covered educational issues for the *Pensacola News Journal*, told me via email. "The complicated part of it was, I do think that parents and community members on both sides thought they were 'keeping children safe,' whether by shielding them from books that didn't align with their own morals, or by giving them freedom to read books widely from various perspectives."

Some parents took more extreme measures. Jennifer Tapley, who was then a school district candidate, turned *Storm and Fury*, Jennifer L. Armentrout's YA novel about a girl who can communicate with ghosts, in to the Santa Rosa County Sheriff's Office. While it had not been subject to a formal challenge, *Storm and Fury*—which had been checked out by a seventeen-year-old student—constituted "child pornography" under Florida House bill

1069, Tapley told a sheriff's deputy. "It's a serious crime," she can be seen arguing on bodycam footage. "It's just as serious as if I handed a *Playboy* to [a minor] right now, right here, in front of you." *Storm and Fury* was subsequently returned to the school, where it was "quarantined" for review.[49]

By the end of 2023, more than 1,600 books, including the *Merriam-Webster* dictionary, had been banned, pending investigation, in Escambia County. Books by Anne Frank, Agatha Christie, Toni Morrison, Jodi Picoult, Cormac McCarthy, Stephen King, Jonathan Franzen, Margaret Atwood, and countless others had been removed, along with *The Guinness World Records* and *Ripley's Believe It or Not!*, for fears they violated Florida's new laws prohibiting sexual material in schools.[50] As for the dictionary, its descriptions of sexual acts might constitute pornography under Florida law.

Many Pensacola parents were appalled by this surge of censorship; some wondered if it was unconstitutional. By early 2024, a U.S. district court judge ruled that Penguin Random House, PEN America, authors, and families in Escambia County had standing to sue. The resulting suit, which is ongoing, alleges that Escambia violated First Amendment rights by removing books "based on ideological objections to their contents or disagreement with their messages or themes," further claiming that "the removals have disproportionately targeted books by or about people of color and / or LGBTQ people."[51]

Lindsay Durtschi, a Pensacola optometrist and mother of two—her Instagram handle is @doctormommyod—remembers the incident that impelled her to join the lawsuit as a plaintiff. A member of the PTA, Durtschi had volunteered to serve on the district's review committee when Raina Telgemeier's graphic novel *Drama* was flagged for LGBTQ "indoctrination." In one scene, a boy in the story confesses to having a crush on another boy. The notion that this amounted to indoctrination, Durtschi felt, was ridiculous.

"I had already read the book with my third grader who loves all of Raina Telgemeier's books," Durtschi recalls. "There was no LGBTQ indoctrination. I still have a straight child as far as I know," she said. Yet here she was, listening to local bigmouths who didn't have children at the school and who possibly hadn't even read the books.* Hearing them fulminate, you'd think Florida was on the cusp of losing a generation of youngsters to sexual pathology.

"It has become tyrannical," Durtschi said of the current atmosphere. "One parent cannot tell me what my kid can read and what my kid can't read, and what is and is not appropriate . . . A lot of the people that are wanting these books to be banned—they don't want their kids and grandkids to know that they were one of the people still throwing stones."

"The problem," she said, "is weak people that are afraid of change."[52]

*   *   *

RIGHT-WING BOOK BANS, rife in Escambia and throughout the South, are the product of a political moment. In the

....

* In Florida's St. Lucie County school district, all seventeen book challenges of the 2021–22 school year were initiated by a sixty-nine-year-old woman named Dale Galiano.

wake of the MAGA movement's dual 2020 loss of both the Trump presidency and the subsequent campaign of election denial, the conservative operative Steve Bannon called for a new electoral strategy.

Bannon believed that Trump had been betrayed by elites within the Republican party. It was now time to flip the script. On his *War Room* podcast, Bannon outlined plans for a MAGA comeback, which would involve seizing control of the apparatus of municipal and state governance from the bottom up. He urged his audience, which can number in the tens of millions, to focus on the lower rungs of American democracy: positions on finance boards, city councils, state legislatures, and libraries.

"It's going to be a fight, but this is a fight that must be won," Bannon declared. "We're going to take this back village by village ... precinct by precinct."[53]

Bannon would devote particular attention to schools. "The path to save the nation is very simple—it's going to go through the school boards," he stated in May 2022.[54] A growing cohort of American parents, Bannon believed, exhausted by the pandemic and the roiling social conflicts of recent years, were fed up with mask mandates, increasingly strident progressive racial politics that upended the nation's founding narratives, and an evolving vocabulary of gender inclusivity that could make your head spin. Schools were where these vectors of outrage converged. They also offered low barriers to entry, democratically speaking: many board positions were not hotly contested, and almost anyone could show up at a school board meeting and command their five minutes of airtime. MAGA Republicans should, as Bannon was fond of saying, "flood the zone."

Bannon was hardly alone in identifying schools as an ideological flashpoint. Throughout these years, conservative parents' rights groups including Moms for Liberty, No Left Turn in Education, MassResistance, and Florida Citizens Alliance arose to confront progressive trends in education, especially those stemming from DEI (diversity, equity, and inclusion). The Florida Citizens Alliance, for instance, opposes sex education in K–12 schools and advocates for the removal of fifty-eight books including *Beloved*, *The Kite Runner*, *The God of Small Things*, and a rhyming children's book called *Everywhere Babies*.[55] The organization's website claims that explicit materials "harm children and potentially groom them to be trafficked."[56] Teachers "can't give a child an aspirin without the parent's permission, yet we can give them this smut and encourage them to be sexually active," said alliance co-founder Keith Flaugh.[57]

No Left Turn defines its mission as "reviving in American education the fundamental discipline of objective thinking...and emphasizing the role of the parent as the primary custodian and authority of their child."[58] They claim to forward a vision of education in which "appreciation of American founding principles is fostered, family values are preserved, and every individual can pursue truth, virtue, beauty and excellence."*

In practice, No Left Turn provides parents (or anyone, really) with a comprehensive toolkit for banning books— resources including lists and form letters targeting texts like *Front Desk*, a middle grade graphic novel about a

---

* You may wonder how an organization devoted to challenging books can simultaneously lay claim to "American founding principles" (including, presumably, free speech). Stay tuned.

Chinese American student living in the motel where her parents work as cleaners. (The author, Kelly Yang, "doesn't miss an opportunity to characterize Caucasian and wealthy people as racist and evil," the letter states.)[59]

Even a small number of committed partisans can generate a staggering volume of challenges to libraries: One man—Bruce Friedman, who leads a Florida chapter of No Left Turn—is responsible for about five hundred complaints in Clay County, where challenged books must be removed from shelves pending review. Friedman's reasons for challenging books include: claims that Donald Trump is a racist; claims that Confederates were pro-slavery; harm being done to human teeth; pentagrams, demons, devils, and ghosts; sexualized youthful banter such as "spank you very much"; wealth redistribution; sexual interactions with aliens, androids, and robots; mentions of mutants; and mentions of Palestine.[60]

* * *

IN APRIL 2023, after a meeting in which board members banned *Lucky* by Alice Sebold and *Push* by Sapphire (both for sexually explicit content), the Escambia Country book challenge process was put on indefinite hold. The reason was not a sudden change of attitude, but rather new legislation which brought even more scrutiny to school libraries throughout the state.

Florida governor Ron DeSantis's Bill 1467 increases citizens' access to the processes by which library books are selected or removed. (The bill was followed, three days later, by the passage of the Parental Rights in Education ["Don't Say Gay"] bill, which prohibited instruction on gender identity and sexual orientation from kindergarten to third grade.) Bill 1467 requires open meetings for selecting instructional materials: Boards must "provide access to all materials," adopt new resources "as a separate line item on the agenda, and provide opportunity for public comment." The Department of Education (DOE) must also publish a list of materials removed "as a result of an objection and disseminate the list to school districts," thereby amplifying individual complaints throughout the entire state.[61]

Each Florida public elementary school now had to publish on its website a list of all its library and classroom books. The bill established new procedures for library acquisitions, stipulating "book selections to be free of pornography." Pornography itself went undefined, although the bill did reference Florida Obscenity Statute 847.012, where pornography also goes undefined, but which describes obscenity as any visual or printed representation of "a person or portion of the human body which depicts nudity or sexual conduct, sexual excitement, sexual battery, bestiality, or sadomasochistic abuse." (Any representation of a nude "portion of the human body," then, is arguably obscene, if not pornographic.) Finally, libraries now had to "provide for the regular removal" of books for various reasons, including "because of an objection by a parent or resident of the county." In short, the bill opened the door to increased book banning by enhancing procedural mechanisms for mounting challenges and then requiring lists of challenged books to be broadcast throughout the state.

Bill 1467 and the Parental Rights in Education Act were important political theatre in what DeSantis was calling "The Year of the Parent." As the governor said in a press release, "This legislation aims to preserve the rights of parents to make decisions about what materials their children are exposed to in school." We often think about "exposure" to asbestos, disease, nuclear fallout, or dodgy men in trench coats; now DeSantis was suggesting that children may be exposed to radioactive words or degenerate ideas.[62]

"In Florida," DeSantis continued, "our parents have every right to be involved in their child's education. We are not going to let politicians deny parents the right to know what is being taught in our schools." DeSantis would have us believe that he is not in favour of book banning; rather, he is merely in favour of parental involvement. He's not denying the rights of children to read certain books; he's holding the line against politicians who would deny parents the right to know what is taught.*

Henceforth, all library materials would be reviewed by an employee "holding a valid education media specialist certificate." The DOE would assure compliance through online training programs. All of this is presented in the banal, administrative, vaguely Orwellian language of the modern professionalized bureaucracy: These were not initiatives of latter-day inquisitors intent on banning books; they were about qualified media specialists performing state-mandated curricular reviews.

But conservative parent groups read between the lines. At least one Orange County mother, Alicia Farrant, was

....

* Did these politicians exist? Was anyone arguing *against* informing parents of the Florida curriculum? Insofar as it was possible to sustain this idea, one of DeSantis's press releases cited a mother in Volusia County who had been barred from a school board meeting for refusing to abide by COVID-era mask mandates.

willing to say the quiet part out loud: "Recently I discovered one of the most disturbing, pornographic books in my child's high school. After some research, I learned that an alarming percentage of high school and middle school library books contain similar material. It is appalling that removal of pornographic and sexually explicit books has even been cause for debate." She was proud to have a governor willing to confront the problem.

Such comments reveal that, beneath the political platitudes, Bill 1467 is not about transparency or grade-appropriate learning. It is about banning "pornography," which constitutes an "alarming percentage" of Florida's library books. Bill 1467 gave book banners the tools to deal with this harmful material.*

Of course, the term "pornography"—along with kindred categories like "obscenity," "indecency," and "scurrilousness"—has no stable, agreed-upon meaning, and often refers to anything deemed threatening to social order. "Obscenity" has changed over time, and so too have the groups most frequently hit with obscenity charges: In 1930s America, 90% of those charged with obscenity were Jewish;[63] more recently, the category became a cudgel with which to attack LGBTQ+ expression. If the last century's worth of First Amendment jurisprudence reveals anything, it is that obscenity and related concepts are notoriously slippery and subject to revision.

....

* Florida Democrats also found use for Bill 1467. In April 2023, minority House leader Fentrice Driskell launched a statewide effort to challenge DeSantis's own book, *The Courage to Be Free*, due to its mentions of critical race theory and LGBTQ+ issues. "The very trap that he set for others is the one that he set for himself," Driskell told *The Daily Beast*, a line worthy of a moustache twirl if there ever was one.

Thankfully, we needn't speculate on what DeSantis meant by the term, because in the spring of 2023, he revealed specific examples of what was now deemed "explicit content" in Florida.

* * *

AT A PRESS conference in Tampa that March, standing behind a podium bearing the phrase EXPOSING THE BOOK BAN HOAX, Ron DeSantis pushed back against the idea that Florida was cracking down on free speech. In the subsequent press release—which carried the warning EXPLICIT CONTENT NOT SUITABLE FOR CHILDREN (necessary, one assumes, to avoid being banned under the censorship regime that he was disavowing as a "hoax")—DeSantis claimed to have "set the record straight, debunking the mainstream media, unions and leftist activists' hoax of empty library bookshelves and political theatre."[64]

Of course, there was no denying that hundreds of books were being pulled from Florida shelves; DeSantis himself was about to produce several examples. In what sense, then, was this a book ban "hoax"?

According to DeSantis, the Florida book ban was a hoax because the materials being banned are not, in fact, books: they are "pornography." True, Mike Curato's autobiographical work, *Flamer*, for instance, gave every impression of being a book; it sounds like one when Curato's publisher describes it as follows: "As Aiden, the main character, navigates friendships, deals with bullies and spends time with Elias (a boy he can't stop thinking about), he finds himself on a path of self-discovery and acceptance." DeSantis, meanwhile, describes *Flamer* as being about "boys performing sexual acts at summer camp." This represents the crude reduction through which gay love becomes obscene, books become less than books, and book bans become liberal hoaxes: remove all narrative context, ignore the author's intentions, and present any non-heterosexual content as purposely corruptive.

DeSantis does not believe that he is limiting children's freedom to read; rather, he is protecting their freedom to read in a pornography-free zone. This is also how parental rights activist groups like No Left Turn can lay claim to the First Amendment while simultaneously working to purge books from school libraries: they refuse to accept that targeted materials count as "books."

"Exposing the 'book ban' hoax is important because it reveals that some are attempting to use our schools for indoctrination," DeSantis said. "In Florida, pornographic and inappropriate materials that have been snuck into our classrooms and libraries to sexualize our students violate our state education standards."[65] Here, DeSantis builds out the mythology underlying his efforts. He specifically alludes to "pornographic" books "snuck into" classrooms and libraries, with the express purpose of "sexualizing" students. Given the other words we have for nefarious people who sneak around sexualizing children—words like "groomer," or "pedophile"—this is starting to sound faintly conspiratorial.* And who is responsible for this sexualization of Florida's children? There can be only one answer.

"Education is about the pursuit of truth," Education Commissioner Manny Diaz Jr. said that day, "not woke

---

* You will recall that the Florida Citizens Alliance warned that pornographic books can "harm children and potentially groom them to be trafficked."

indoctrination." Finally, our true culprit comes fully into view: the "woke." The libs.

But this is not Ben Shapiro or Alex Jones. This is the governor of Florida using official state channels to tiptoe right up to the idea that woke groomers have infiltrated school libraries in order to corrupt children. Only those suffering under LGBTQ+ indoctrination could interpret DeSantis's actions to save children as a book ban. No, this wasn't about banning books: it was about saving children from sexually deviant propaganda.

* * *

BACK IN MAY 2022, I had only a vague sense of what was happening in Florida, although I worried—in the wake of the "library audit" announcement—that censorship of a different stripe was coming for our school. Was "audit" not precisely the sort of dry, procedural word that would conceal the arrival of book banning in Toronto's schools? I intended to find out.

Our principal, a short-haired woman with bright, statement-making glasses, made no secret of the fact that a good many of our library books were "problematic." By way of example, she showed the parent committee a non-descript picture book about a family. We looked at it for a few moments, uncomprehendingly, before the principal pointed out that the child in the book was depicted as having a female mother and a male father. They were also white. Was the implicit message here not that "normal" families had two straight, white parents? Would BIPOC children not feel pointedly excluded by such representation of family life?

The real problem, the principal said with mild exasperation, was that the library was *full* of this stuff. This was when she said that, were it up to her, we would just get rid of "all the old books."

After some further preliminaries it was time to begin our investigation. The other volunteers and I were asked to select just five books, mostly at random, which we would then adjudicate using the TDSB Equity Toolkit as a guide.

The toolkit consists of seventeen yes or no questions intended to guide the selection of educational books from a "Culturally Relevant and Responsive stance." I cracked open my first selection—a tender, illustrated children's book called *Suki's Kimono*, about a Japanese girl who wears her ancestral dress on the first day of school—and got to work. First question: "Does the text reflect students' social identities, histories, and experiences?" I wasn't sure. Clearly, it depended upon which students you meant. Japanese students might see themselves reflected in *Suki's Kimono* or they might groan at the stereotypical signifiers of Japanese culture (sōmen noodles, taiko drummers, or the kimono itself). Regardless, the vast majority of students in our Greektown neighbourhood would not see their "social identities, histories, and experiences" reflected in *Suki's Kimono*, so the honest answer was no.

Down the checklist I went. "Does the text build on students' experiences in ways that promote well-being and belonging?" Again, it was difficult to answer in the absence of specific students and experiences, so I could not definitively say yes. Next question: "Does the text tap into students' interests?" In aggregate, probably not.

"Does the text silence or omit certain groups or topics?" Reluctantly, I supposed it did: there were no Black or Indigenous voices in *Suki's Kimono*; in Equity Toolkit terms, they had at least been "omitted." It wasn't looking good for *Suki's Kimono*.

Several of the questions struck me as vague, as though intended to provide auditors with maximal discretion. Was the text "accessible to all students?" No, and how could *any* book be accessible to *all* students? "Consider the perspective, beliefs, and identities of the author." But I didn't know the first thing about Chieri Uegaki. I could have started combing through the author's biography and social media feeds, but I remain sympathetic to W. K. Wimsatt and Monroe Beardsley's "The Intentional Fallacy," the famous 1946 essay in which they argue that "the intention of the author is neither available nor desirable as a standard for judging the success of a work of literary art."

Of course—and here's the rub—the Equity Toolkit didn't see children's literature as "works of literary art." Its binary "yes or no" questions seem formulated to identify books as good (texts that "provide opportunities for students to challenge the status quo" and "offer students an extension to act in response to injustice") or bad (texts that "reinforce, perpetuate, or highlight stereotypes and/or misrepresent specific groups and identifies"). Yet all of these concepts struck me as inherently fraught. *Suki's Kimono* highlighted an ambiguity between cultural signifiers and stereotypes: the indications of Japanese culture seemed appropriate enough to me, but it was also possible that, to some Japanese students, they might present as fixed or oversimplified images of their culture—in other words, as stereotypes. Which authority would properly adjudicate this matter? The author? The Japanese students, with their varying possible reactions? Me, with my checklist?

This might have sparked an interesting classroom conversation about the ethics of imagination. But the cumulative effect of the toolkit, it seemed to me, was to boil away the imaginative quality of children's stories and treat them as vehicles for politically coded messages. Its questions assume that the purpose of reading is the affirmation of identity, and the affirmation of identity promotes "well-being." Literature, in the toolkit's terms, is valuable insofar as it "combats oppression" through this therapeutic function, fostering respect, belonging, and a positive self-image. These are laudable aims. Of course, almost no serious literature (from Homer to Toni Morrison) is defensible in terms of depicting or encouraging "healthy human relationships." Many of the world's best plays end with a pile of corpses on the floor. Entire prose genres may be disqualified by such criteria.

The Equity Toolkit also makes several assumptions about readerly identification. Several of its questions refer to "building on student experiences," tapping into their "prior knowledge," offering students "mirrors into themselves," and so on. This form of identification, and the solace it can provide, can be an extraordinary, transcendental gift for readers. "When I say that I am alive because queer books like *We Are Okay* saved me, I mean every word," writes Leslie Lopez, a queer woman who struggled to find affirmation in her religious Southern family.[66] We must hear students who emphasize the transformative impact of finding themselves in literature, and ensure that this form of literary engagement is open to all.

But there are other forms of literary engagement—not better but different. Literature is, among other things, a medium for young people to transcend their quotidian reality, generating encounters with a range of lived and unlived experience. Children are avid for knowledge of the world beyond their immediate purview. Grade six students don't want to live in a cultural space limited to the experience of eleven-year-olds. Nor will their imaginations necessarily conform to specific identity categories. Peel educators were instructed to undertake a "representation audit" of their libraries, which provided the following boxes for each literary character: Asian, Black, Christian, Hindu, Indigenous, Jewish, Latinx, Muslim, Sikh, Tamil, White, 2SLGBTQ+, and "other characters." Some students may see themselves reflected in these categories. Others may see themselves in different terms—as survivors, as people with disabilities, as caregivers. Some see themselves as leaders, athletes, musicians, gamers, coders, or identify with visions of their imagined future selves—their ambitions to become influencers or NBA players or millionaires or the creators of a green-tech start-up, or any of the other infinite ways in which people see themselves. Each of us have aspects of our identities that are projected onto us by others, and aspects which we choose for ourselves—traits or dreams with which we actively *identify*. Literature needn't privilege one form of identity over the other: Indeed, it is perhaps the best vehicle human beings have devised for bridging identities.

Affirmation—of any sort—is not the uncontested goal of literary study. Sometimes, readers should leave a text feeling *unsettled* rather than affirmed. Sometimes, students should be confronted with unfamiliar experiences, along with familiar ones, and engage in liberating flights of imaginative fancy that leave their earthbound identities far behind. And they should be taught the art and artifice of narrative strategy, the ways in which the portrayal of any "self" or "identity" in literature is the product of identifiable formal conventions and techniques, the ways in which older and even ancient archetypes underlie our most contemporary stories, and so on.

There are many alternative frameworks for selecting educational texts, as well as more thought-provoking questions for students and teachers to ask. In their 2008 book, *Good Books Matter: How to choose and use children's literature to help students grow as readers*, Shelley Stagg Peterson and Larry Swartz encouraged teachers to pose a variety prompts, such as "What images are created in your mind as you read the story?" and "Why do you think the author chose to write from the point of view of ____?"

These words—"point of view," "image," "story"—as well as others I've been using—"imagination," "character," "theme," "technique"—are some foundational terms of literary study, but none appear on the TDSB checklist. That is because the checklist exists not to promote the understanding of literature but to further an ideological program. That program claims an all-encompassing authority. Every children's book—from Dr. Seuss's *The Cat in the Hat* to Robert Munsch's *Love You Forever*—needs to provide an equity-based accounting of itself. Do Grimm's fairy tales encourage students to "respond to injustice"? Does *Where the Sidewalk Ends* interrupt hate? The more I thought about the Equity Toolkit, the more convinced I became that its questions mostly evaded the literary qualities of literature, and that educators who want to do justice to their subject—and their students—will have to look elsewhere.

* * *

TIME WAS UP. I was supposed to review five books in the time provided but hadn't progressed beyond *Suki's Kimono*. Sitting in a chair designed for an elementary student, my knees up around my ears, I explained that I had made a good-faith effort to use the toolkit but found the questions too abstract to be helpful. Everything hinged upon how the texts were positioned and taught by educators.

As it turned out, my fellow inquisitors had quickly bailed on their toolkits. They'd picked a question or two, or scanned their books for racist or stereotypical images. In the end, our volunteer group agreed that students of every race and gender should be able to access stories that speak to their identity—and the way to do so was by adding books, rather than purging them. Even then, however, I wondered if the chronic underfunding of schools and libraries could make the adding of books seem less feasible than culling them.

Walking home, I was uncertain about what we were supposed to have accomplished. Our committee had spent about two hours discussing a small handful of books—a tiny fraction of the library's holdings. At one point, the principal implied that the purpose of the exercise was to educate *us*—the parents who were assisting with the process. Perhaps, newly converted, we would bring the equity perspective to bear on our books at home.

While I left feeling hopeful that the books we'd examined would not be pulled from the shelves, it was clear that the censorship apparatus—along with the belief that literature exists to service a political agenda—had taken root. The subjective criteria offered by the Equity Toolkit could be used to challenge almost any classic of children's literature. I also wondered if the pruning might continue behind closed doors, with teachers and staff in the role of inquisitors. Parents had no way of knowing what was on the shelves, or what might quietly disappear.

But this was Toronto, not Florida. Book banning was still something that happened elsewhere.

* * *

IN SEPTEMBER 2023, a grade ten student named Reina Takata entered the library of Erindale Secondary School in Mississauga, just west of Toronto, for the first time that year. Reina knew the library well; she ate her lunch there most days. But on this day she was stunned by what she saw.

"This year, I came into my school library and there are rows and rows of empty shelves with absolutely no books," Takata said. She estimated that more than 50% of the school's library holdings had vanished. The CBC reported that this extensive pruning was part of "a new equity-based book weeding process implemented by the board." This process, "intended to ensure library books are inclusive, appears to have led some schools to remove thousands of books solely because they were published in 2008 or earlier."*[67]

....

* On the question of why the fifteen-year weeding cut-off was chosen, an internal training manual cites the importance of relevant and "culturally responsive" material. The answer goes on to emphasize "anti-racism and anti-oppression" in ensuring "a fair and equitable process for the removal of texts."

After the news broke, Ontario's education minister, Stephen Lecce, ordered the Peel District School Board (PDSB) to halt the weeding process. In response, the board said that older books would be permitted to remain in school libraries that had yet to undertake the purges, so long as those books were "accurate, relevant to the student population, inclusive, not harmful, and support the current curriculum." Even in accepting the directive to stop their expurgation of pre-2008 library books, the board was claiming extraordinary leeway to continue culling as they saw fit.

Predictably, removing books based on their publication date brought perverse side effects. In the name of inclusion, Anne Frank's *Diary* had been weeded from the shelves. As student Reina Takata, who is of Japanese descent, observed: "I think that authors who wrote about Japanese internment camps are going to be erased and that the entire events that went on historically for Japanese Canadians are going to be removed."[68]

Reading about the book purges in Peel Region, I couldn't help but recall how our principal had mused about eliminating "all the old books." Peel Region, too, concluded that many older books were irredeemably problematic. They seemed to believe that student reading should take place in a perpetual present. Insofar as history would be available, it would be filtered through the educational priorities of our moment, without the encumbrances of primary texts and their complicating, sometimes contradictory evidence.

Because the culled books were "causing harm," librarians were forbidden from donating them to charity. An internal training document, "Weeding and Audit Resources in the Library Learning Commons Collection," called these books a "health hazard." In addition to potentially containing mould, "They are not inclusive, culturally responsive, relevant or accurate (racism, stereotypes, microaggression, lack of representation or erasure of communities, slurs, oppression, etc.)." Educators were explicitly told that "de-selected resources must be disposed of immediately," and that they "should be packed up in such a way that they cannot be accessed again and to prevent relocation."[69] The books were put in garbage bins and sent to the dump.[70]

The Peel Region "book weeding" directive applied to 259 schools. Some of them threw out thousands of books. The total number is unknowable.[71]

* * *

IN THE WAKE of the equity-based book purge, some teacher librarians described their work to the media. Evelyn Reford weeded just over 2,000 of the 6,500 books in her library. "Although I understand people's emotional reaction to the idea of books being taken from libraries," Reford told the CBC, "they're only being taken from libraries because they're not serving the population anymore." Reford didn't explain what "serving the population" means—her choice of that formulation over "serving the students" suggests a census-based approach to literary quality—but one can only assume, based on training materials, that the purged materials (including Eric Carle's *The Very Hungry Caterpillar*) were insufficiently identity-affirming.

Other teacher librarians found the process to be rushed and unclear and felt pressured to remove large numbers of books. "It's hard to see these books that you love be thrown away," said one, who removed about 20% of her collection. "The hardest part was some of the non-fiction books, like some of the animal books. I didn't quite understand why I had to get rid of those."[72]

After the story broke, the board claimed that it would pursue its equity goals through the addition of books. "Despite potential cutbacks," said Paul Da Silva, associate director for school improvement and equity, "really what this has done is highlighted the importance of maintaining fulsome libraries." One teacher librarian said that she had received only a fraction of the money required to restock the shelves. "It's going to take a lot of money to basically replenish what we've lost—because we lost a lot," she said.

Bernadette Smith, a board superintendent, explained that equity-based weeding would continue. "We want to ensure that when a student picks up a book that it's not causing harm," said Smith. Confronted with the spectre of half-empty shelves, she said, "It's not about the quantity of the books, it's about the quality."[73]

* * *

FLORIDA AND ONTARIO have distinct political cultures, and nowhere are those differences more pronounced than in education. Florida's schools remained open for in-person learning throughout much of the pandemic; Ontario's were closed for twenty-seven weeks over three school years, longer than almost anywhere else. While Ron DeSantis attempted to ban the teaching of concepts related to racism, gender, and privilege with his "Stop WOKE Act," Ontario educators revised their curricula to foreground these very subjects. Yet different as they are, both jurisdictions have seen the arrival of book banning as a means of enforcing ideological conformity.

The banners differ in their methods and goals. Florida's began with parental advocacy groups; Ontario's originated from within its institutions. Florida's book banning unfolds in raucous marathon meetings of local school boards. Ontario's unfolds under a cloak of secrecy: students return to discover that their libraries had been noticeably emptied. Conservative Floridians cite LGBTQ+ indoctrination; progressive Ontarians cite inclusivity and identity affirmation. But in the end, both resort to the same tactic, and for the same reason: to "save children from harm."

Book banners in Florida and Ontario exemplify the new censorship consensus. It proceeds from the righteous conviction that, so extraordinary are the dangers posed by our enemies (whether those enemies are populists or woke, communists or racists), we must extirpate harmful books before they corrupt our children. Its defensive rhetoric cloaks its offensive intentions, justifying the symbolic violence it projects onto that which it deems intolerable.

Neither side will own up to the word "censorship." Indeed, a Peel Region training document provides teacher librarians with talking points to defuse this touchy subject: "The texts that are weeded are not labelled as 'bad' or 'banned' but are rather deemed unsuitable for the student learning community as they are not student-centered [and] identity-affirming...It is essential to remove texts that perpetuate harm and oppression."[74] Yet the board's actions clearly constitute censorship according to the definition provided by the Ontario School Library Association (OSLA): "censorship is the removal, suppression, or restricted circulation" of materials "because they are morally or otherwise objectionable." Adds the OSLA: "While the selector seeks reasons to include material in the collection, the censor seeks reasons to exclude material from the group."[75] Any toolkit or manual intended to expedite the removal or restriction of library books is, according to the OSLA's own definition, designed to facilitate censorship.

Parental rights advocates are similarly loathe to identify as censors or banners. Keith Flaugh, of the Florida Citizens Alliance, finds the term "book ban" to be "incendiary" and unhelpful (he prefers "prohibited"). "This is really about protecting our children and keeping the harmful materials from them just like we do drugs and cigarettes," Flaugh said.[76]

No one, it seems, self-identifies as a book banner—not even those working to remove books from libraries. The DeSantis supporter takes refuge in the knowledge that she is not pro–book banning, just anti-pornography, while the progressive educator knows that she is not pro–book banning, just anti-racist.

But by removing and destroying books to prevent harm to children, today's censors are, ironically, creating whole new sources of harm. Book banning harms some children by depriving them of information or narratives that may have enriched their lives. It harms others by whitewashing or severing them from history and presenting a sanitized version of reality. It impairs their development as democratic citizens, teaching them that, when confronted with a disagreeable or upsetting viewpoint, the solution is to ban, silence, or prohibit. It represents lost moral or educational opportunities: By preventing students from thinking through their own responses to difficult material, censorship also prevents them from discovering why they think what they do. It encourages students to conceive of themselves as passive receptacles of material that may corrupt or traumatize them—the very opposite of resilient.

Book banning limits students' relationship to art and literature by encouraging a purely mimetic mindset ("text as mirrors") and by discouraging an understanding of art as artifice, the product of formal conventions and techniques. Book banning is demeaning to young people: It assumes they can't understand how language and social norms have evolved over time, and treats history as dangerous and unteachable. It lies to them by implying that they may be "indoctrinated" into adopting an LGBTQ+ identity by reading a book, or into holding the wrong views. Where the teaching of literacy should involve the cultivation of critical faculties, censorship strips students of their own agency and judgment in confronting ideas they may find challenging.

Book banning is a form of coercion, an attempt to control not only what children read, but also what they think. Left unchecked, it poses two longer-term dangers. The first is that students will become habituated to the conditions of censorship. They will grow up to be uninformed and passive, easier targets for propaganda and (actual) indoctrination, primed for authoritarian rule. The second is that they will internalize the methods of their censorious parents and educators and organize their own lives around a will to power. They will *become* the censors and the authoritarians.

To turn the tide in schools, we need to persuade parents and educators that it is the banners themselves, not the books, who are the true sources of harm. We must also educate students on the harms of censorship, and on the reasons why expressive freedom, and its underlying promise of individual autonomy, are fundamental values that we cannot live without. That education begins with the long, sordid history of censorship in the West, which is the subject of our next chapter.

2. Paranoid, Righteous, and Perverse: Two Thousand Years of Censorship in the West

THE HISTORY OF censorship is older than the novel, older than the printed word, older than democracy, older than history. The instinct to silence our rivals, to still the tongues of those we find threatening or disgusting, is ancient and unassuageable. We moderns want to believe that self-expression is the essence of our humanity, but the opposite is just as true. History has been shaped and pared by an impulse to silence the expression of the disagreeable Other. Certainly, since the advent of free speech in ancient Athens, censorship has been the rule, and expressive freedom the exception.

One of those exceptional periods unfolded in ancient Rome, early in the reign of Julius Caesar. For a time, Caesar governed by rhetoric rather than force, permitting oral and written criticism and responding in kind. After becoming consul in 59 BCE, Caesar published the proceedings of senatorial meetings: these reports, the *acta senatus*, were published in the *populi acta diurnal*, often described as the world's first newspaper.

Things changed under Augustus, Rome's first emperor. After consolidating power in 27 BCE, Augustus adopted a less transparent policy, publishing only excerpts of senatorial debates, those sufficiently flattering to his imperial government. But Augustus was to go much further in the direction of censorship. Like many tyrants since, he felt he had no choice.

His first targets were prophets. Oracles and astrological interpreters were a particular nuisance for Roman authorities, given to prophesying the demise of the regime. (There was always a robust market for forecasts of revolution.) Augustus moved to classify such prophesy as a species of insurrectionary dissent. In 12 BCE, he decreed all oracular scrolls, pamphlets, and books to be incinerated in an auto-da-fé. Some two thousand publications were gathered up and torched in the first official book burning in Roman history. Before long, even pro-government prophesies—predictions of the empire's greater glory—were enough to get you flung from the twenty-five-metre-high Tarpeian Rock, along with murderers and traitors, or flogged and beheaded to the sound of trumpets outside the Esquiline Gate.

Still, Augustus was apprehensive. As time passed, circumstances convinced him to broaden the scope of material fit for the pyre.

Between the years 6 and 8 CE, Rome was stricken with inflation. Grain prices shot up, bread rations were imposed, but Romans were starving. As the famine spread, so too did criticism of Augustus's rule. Influential citizens would wake up to find anonymously written anti-government tracts nailed to their doors. The emperor's closest advisers urged him to choke off dissent: failure to act against this unruly speech, they said, would spell the end of his rule.

Augustus decided to clamp down. He adapted two traditional prohibitions—one, a Twelve Table law against defamatory writings; the other, *lex maiestatis*, crimes against the emperor—to create a new legal tool: literary treason. This novel crime brought a novel punishment— the literary death sentence. "In milder cases, some works of a guilty author might be sentenced to the stake; in graver ones, his whole life-work would be committed to the flames," writes the Classics scholar Frederick Cramer. "It was not long until the next logical steps were taken: private possession of condemned writings became a crime, and so did the very reading of some of them."[77]

Professors were among the first to fall afoul of the new law. Titus Labienus, a peppery critic of the Augustan order, was convicted by the Senate and saw his life's work consigned to flames. He took his own life, but not before ensuring that he wouldn't be cremated, as though to spite the fiery element that had consumed his work.[78]

Then there was the pathetic case of the poet Clutorius Priscus. In 19 CE, Emperor Tiberius (Augustus's heir) engaged Clutorius to write an elegy for his nephew, who had died at a tender age. (Poison was suspected.) Shortly thereafter, Tiberius's son, Drusus, became seriously ill. Clutorius, sniffing another payday, decided to get a head start on his elegy. His mistake—a fatal one, as it would turn out—was to recite the poem to a small audience. Drusus not only recovered; he presided over Clutorius's trial for literary treason, where the poet was found guilty and summarily executed.[79] ·

Finally, there was the elderly historian, Aulus Cremutius Cordus, who was hauled before the Senate for allegedly treasonous passages in his *Annals*. As the Roman historian Cassius Dio recorded: "Cordus was accused of having praised Cassius and Brutus," architects of the assassination of Julius Caesar, and "while he had spoken no ill of them [Emperors Augustus and Tiberius], he had not, on the other hand, shown any unusual respect for them." The Senate decreed that Cordus's books were to be burned. Unable to go on, the great historian starved himself to death.[80]

Within three generations, Rome had mutated or pupated from a polis in which dissent was tolerated into one where insufficiently glowing histories of the empire were burned—where poets of questionable political instincts were sacrificed in murderous spectacles. A brief, exceptional period of freedom had ended, and the rule of censorship returned to Rome.

* * *

IN ADDITION TO book burnings, and the exile and execution of authors, ancient Romans had another potent tool in their censorship arsenal: memory sanctions. One of the earliest known forms of state-sponsored censorship, the practices scholars now refer to as *damnatio memoria*—literally, a damning of one's memory—occurred when the Senate voted to obliterate all trace of a Roman noble. This might be a traitor or conspirator, a disloyal relative of the emperor, or a discredited emperor himself: Caligula, Nero, and Domitian were among the disavowed emperors who suffered memory sanctions. *Damnatio memoria* had been around for centuries, practised among aristocratic families of the Republic and Hellenistic kings who glorified themselves by wiping previous rulers from the public record.

For a society obsessed with shared memory and commemoration, the prospect of total erasure was an ultimate form of retribution. The Roman elite's belief in its own ability to cleanse the public memory serves, as scholar Harriet I. Flower argues, "to assert the power of the community over its own narrative and, therefore, over its present and future direction."[81] The targets of such sanctions had their names expunged from public documents and institutional records, their images destroyed, their books burned and their laws revoked. Their coins were melted down, statues toppled, names chiselled out of monuments, homes flattened. If the sanctions were applied in time, there would be no funeral for the damned, no marker of his grave. He would simply cease to be.

Except that it was never that simple, as Roman citizens still had their personal memories of those who had been scrubbed from the official record. Gashing someone's name out of a stone monument doesn't undo the past, but it does create a new kind of absence, with its own kind of power: the power inherent in those whose names are unsayable, who have driven the state to mutilate itself. Memory sanctions thus "appear to flow freely between extremes of oblivion and disgrace," Flower writes, "in a dynamic memory space shaped in part by shame and silence, but in part also by vituperation and ongoing debate about the merits or vices of the deceased."[82] The history of *damnatio memoria* reveals how, even in the relatively stable, pre-digital world, censorship rarely functioned in a predictable way. It created new absences, silences to be filled with debate. There were about seventy Roman emperors in this period, but some of the ones we know best suffered memory sanctions.

*   *   *

ANCIENT ROME GAVE the Western world some of its first public libraries, which were often adjacent to baths.* The *thermae*, an innovation of Nero (reign 54–68 CE), were hubs for networking and cultural exchange, and became sites of reading. By 350 CE there were perhaps thirty such libraries in the city of Rome.

Romans of social standing had long maintained private *bibliotheca*, stocked with wax tablets and papyrus rolls; some early bibliophiles adorned them with cover pages (*syllabi*). Roman elites were known to maintain two or three separate libraries, for Latin, Greek, and other languages, equipped with staff for arranging and maintaining the contents. Romans expanded their libraries through military spoils, purchases from merchants, or transcribing texts from other libraries. The stoic philosopher Seneca disparaged these elaborate collections, insisting that it was pure vanity to own more than you could read in your lifetime. Private libraries were status symbols—familiarity with Greek literature was a particular mark of distinc-

....

* Private collections date back to the ancient Greeks. Aristotle is sometimes identified as the first serious collector. Historical repositories of written material extend back to Sumer, the earliest known civilization, in 3400 BCE.

tion—but they were more than that. History is full of friendships that unfolded over the borrowing of books.[83]

Most of these Roman libraries were destroyed—many by fire (caused by lightning, fumbled torches, or arson), and many more sacked by Goths. For much of military history, plundering or destroying your opponents' libraries was standard operating procedure. So frequent was the intentional destruction of libraries that the scholar Rebecca Knuth coined a useful term for it: *libricide*. Roman emperors ordered the destruction of Christian libraries; then, as Christianity arose to greater power, early popes ordered the destruction of Roman literature. Pope Gregory I, a future saint, ordered the destruction of every extant copy of works by Cicero, Livy, and others.

The most important library of the ancient world, in Alexandria, Egypt, stood for some seven hundred years. By the third century BCE, the Great Library of Alexandria held some five hundred thousand scrolls and countless other monuments to human culture. It provided an intellectual home to revolutionary scholars including Archimedes, who laid the groundwork for modern calculus; Eratosthenes of Cyrene, who determined that the earth is round, calculating its diameter to within eighty kilometres of the number we now know to be correct; Aristarchus of Samos, who theorized a heliocentric solar system nearly two millennia before Copernicus; and Aristophanes of Byzantium, who divided poetry into lines. "Alexandria was a place where what could be known of Babylonian, Egyptian, Jewish, and Greek thought was strenuously collected, codified, systematized, and contained," Roy MacLeod writes. It was "the foundation of the text-centered culture of the Western tradition."[84]

No one knows exactly who destroyed the Great Library. In his *History of the Decline and Fall of the Roman Empire*, Edward Gibbon pins the blame on Theophilus, the Patriarch of Alexandria, and his Christian zealots, who "pillaged or destroyed" the library's contents in 391 CE. Gibbon imagines the profound "regret and indignation" experienced by anyone of sound mind (that is, whose mind "was not totally darkened by religious prejudice") when confronted with those shelves, now emptied of invaluable monuments to science and literacy.[85]

Modern historians don't buy Gibbon's account. Some believe that much of the library's contents had already been consumed by fire, or point to Emperor Caracalla's rampage through Alexandria during the Parthian campaign of 216 CE. Whatever remained of the Great Library was probably extinguished according to Caliph Omar's orders in the Arab conquest of 641 CE: "If the content of the books is in accordance with the book of Allah, we may do without them, for in that case, the book of Allah more than suffices. If, on the other hand, they contain matter not in accordance with the book of Allah there can be no need to preserve them. Proceed, then, and destroy them."

The final remnants of the ancient world's capital of knowledge and learning were shovelled into the stoves that warmed the public baths. There were enough pages from the Great Library of Alexandria to keep the fires going for six months, and then they were gone.[86]

* * *

THE GREAT LIBRARIES of today will be destroyed tomorrow: This is the final lesson of the Library of Pergamum in what is now Turkey, the House of Wisdom in Iraq, the Imperial Library of Constantinople. After the Warsaw uprising, the Nazis burned the National Library of Poland. In the War of 1812, the British burned the American Library of Congress. The Lebanese National Library, the National Library of Cambodia, the National and University Library of Bosnia and Herzegovina—ashes. A full accounting of the censorship and destruction of Chinese and Russian books would require books of their own.

Millenia from now, if humanity endures, historians will consult *their* libraries in debates about who was to blame for the destruction of *our* libraries—who lit the flame, who smashed the idols, whose God demanded violent propitiation, who fed the books into the furnaces. But the fact of their destruction will not be debated.

* * *

CENSORSHIP EVOLVES ALONGSIDE technological innovation, and no technological innovation was more revolutionary than the printing press. In hindsight, we can see how the spread of print technology in fifteenth- and sixteenth-century Europe set off cascading social revolutions. As Benedict Anderson shows in *Imagined Communities*, the dissemination of print media—newspapers, pamphlets, and literature—contributed to the rise of literacy in the vernacular languages (e.g., English and French, the languages people actually spoke, unlike Latin), creating an imagined community of readers. That community, which became the modern nation, would spell the end of the feudal-dynastic order—but not before extraordinarily bloody wars of religion consumed much of Europe throughout the sixteenth and seventeenth centuries.* These conflicts were fuelled by the profusion of unauthorized religious treatises, commentaries, confessional documents, and translations that poured from the continent's printing presses. Such texts allowed individual readers to interrogate theological ideas for themselves; they also hastened the splintering of rival sects that broke off from the Church of Rome, and then from each other.

Just as social media companies have made the urgent case for content moderation in our time, so, too, did Church authorities feel compelled to clamp down on heretical disinformation. They bemoaned the spread of superstition and worried about the erosion of ecclesiastical authority—mirroring our own epistemic crisis, in which people are said to exist within their own algorithmically determined reality fields. Protestant monarchs took up censorship in their turn, passing new requirements for pre-publication licences. King Henry VIII empowered the Court of Star Chamber to censor printed material; Elizabeth I gave censorship power to the Archbishops of Canterbury and York. No book was to be published without their assent, and the penalty for slandering or dishonouring the Queen's Majesty was the loss of the right hand.[87] Still, unauthorized texts continued to circulate.

If the arrival of the printing press presented an existential problem for Early Modern religious authorities, censorship was their solution. And of all the institutional efforts to police books over the ensuing half millennium, none was more exhaustive and far-reaching than the

....

* These wars involved political and economic factors, as well as religious ones, and alliances weren't always sectarian. The sack of Rome in 1527, for instance, saw Lutherans fighting alongside Catholic soldiers in the Imperial army.

Roman Catholic Church's *Index librorum prohibitorum*, or Index of Prohibited Books.

* * *

THE ROMAN CATHOLIC Church's Index of Prohibited Books was astonishingly ambitious: As Robin Vose argues in his impressive study of the subject, its goal was nothing less than "absolute control over the spiritual and ideological content of written and other forms of communication that audiences of the faithful might be exposed to throughout their lives."

The first *Index librorum prohibitorum*, published in 1557, grew out of localized lists of contraband books that had been proliferating in Europe for decades. A precursor had been produced by an alliance of Dutch university professors in the 1530s. State power has, of course, always sought to control the flow of information: Michel Foucault famously argued that the very idea of authorship grew out of the state's need to punish individuals as the source of seditious ideas.

Those in power in the sixteenth century, especially in the Roman Catholic world, had grounds for concern. The Protestant Reformation and incipient print culture had ensured mass circulation of subversive ideas. The Catholic Church's Index intended to compile, in one volume, a list of heretical books and authors that were corrosive to the faith of all but the most specialized readers. At its height, the Index ran some 1,400 dense pages, plus sheaths of supplemental edicts. It would have been years out of date by the time it arrived in the hands of those charged with carrying out the censorship.

In bookshop raids and cargo inspections alike, unauthorized Bibles and scriptural commentaries (including
Protestant contraband) were first to be summarily confiscated and burned; also high on the list were works involving
alchemy and Freemasonry, and those of Catholic dissidents.
Later targets included scientists (Galileo, Copernicus),
political theorists (Hobbes, Locke, Adam Smith), philosophers (Rousseau, Hume, Kant), scores of writers (Alexandre
Dumas, Victor Hugo), and countless theologians. Had those
behind the Index succeeded, works by these authors would
have been scrubbed from human history.*

The Church was hardest on its own. Giordano Bruno
was a sixteenth-century Dominican friar with a habit of
attracting the wrong kind of attention. Once, Bruno's mas-
ters discovered that he had concealed a volume by Erasmus,
a prohibited Dutch theologian, in the monastery toilets.
But Bruno's bathroom reading would turn out to be the
least of his heresies. In his later career as a mathematician
and theologian, he espoused controversial ideas including
what we now call the Copernican model of the universe,
with its implication that we are not the centre of God's
creation. Bruno speculated that other planets could support life of their own, and wrote sacrilegious books (with
provocative titles like *Theses on Magic*) which drew the
attention of Roman inquisitors. In February 1600, Bruno's
luck finally ran dry; he was bound, gagged, and burned at
a wooden stake.[88]

Mostly, however, Church censors thought of their
work less in the negative terms of punishing heretics than

....

* In practice, civil governments (especially in states like Florence and Ven-
  ice, the latter of which had a flourishing book trade) were sometimes less
  than perfectly cooperative in matters of censorship.

in the positive light of saving souls. Vose likens the work of the Congregation of the Index to that of the peer review function of scholarship, fact-checking in journalism, or content moderation: It was intended to promote "honest discernment of good from bad spiritual, intellectual, literary and cultural productions—in modern terms, by distinguishing between art and trash, debunking 'junk' science and charlatans, muting 'fake news,' and so on."

For the most part, those tasked with assigning books to the Index were highly learned biblical scholars who took their work seriously. Debates over some texts could stretch on for years, and often involved fine-grained theological distinctions. For instance, the *De auxiliis* question of whether good works on earth might get you into heaven became so controversial that Pope Clement VIII declared the entire topic off limits.

The Index brought no shortage of perverse and even humorous outcomes. In 1627, the chief librarian of Oxford's Bodleian used it as a bibliographical wish list to guide acquisitions and encouraged other librarians to do the same. So handy was the Index for Protestants that they started printing it themselves, often with cheeky prefatory notes mocking the Catholic censors. The Congregation responded by adding these illicit Protestant Indexes to their own future Indexes.

The Index nevertheless wrought unfathomable harm on human creativity over the course of centuries. One can only speculate about the books that weren't written, the discoveries that weren't disseminated, the artists and thinkers who censored themselves and deprived history of what might have been. In colonial contexts, the Church-endorsed work of censorship became sanctified vandalism.

"Despite its lack of formal appearance in the Indexes," Vose writes, "censorship of both Indigenous and spiritual texts and translations into Indigenous languages would be one of the most long-lasting harms ever inflicted by the Catholic Church upon the New World."

Given the sheer magnitude of effort required to monitor the cultural production of all humanity, it's amazing how long the Index lasted. It ended in 1966, under Pope Paul VI, not because of any doctrinal shift on the part of the Church, but because the pace of human culture had finally made it impossible to keep up.

* * *

WHILE THE INDEX *librorum prohibitorum* remains the most enduring institutional approach to cultural surveillance and control, determined individuals have also played an outsized role in the history of censorship. One of those individuals was Anthony Comstock, an American whose very name was to become synonymous with his life's mission: the suppression of vice.

Born in 1844 in New Canaan, Connecticut, Comstock served in the Union Army during the American Civil War. What impressed itself most indelibly upon his conscience, however, was not the staggering bloodshed of that conflict, which claimed an estimated 620,000 souls, but rather the foul language of his fellow soldiers—men also disposed to drinking, smoking, and enjoying lascivious books like *Pictures for Bachelors* and *Bedroom Photographs for Gentlemen Only*. Comstock became quite unpopular for his constant evangelizing and pestering the company to join prayer meetings. "Seems to be a feeling of hatred by some of the boys," he mused in an 1864 diary entry. "Can I sacrifice Principle and conscience for Praise of Man? *Never*."[89]

The Civil War ended before he saw action, but Comstock's war was just beginning. After spearheading the New York City YMCA's anti-vice efforts, he created the Society for the Suppression of Vice. His methods were straightforward: using an alias, he would send off for sexually explicit materials—racy half-dime novels, photographs with "fancy views," phallic drinking vessels, condoms made of fish bladder, and other "aids to seduction"—and then seek the arrest of anyone who provided them. Because he believed such materials could corrupt the minds of the jury, he often incinerated evidence prior to trial, leaving jurors dependent upon his descriptions of the contraband.[90]

Comstock evolved into a relentless crusader for public morals, once trailing a suspect from Connecticut to New York, Montreal, Detroit, Chicago, St. Louis, New Orleans, and finally to Philadelphia, all because the man had sold him a condom.[91]

In 1873, Comstock lobbied Washington for a new federal law to crack down on obscenity. To emphasize the urgency of such legislation, he exhibited items from his "Chamber of Horrors." Sufficiently impressed, Congress passed the "Act for the Suppression of Trade in, and Circulation of, Obscene Literature and Articles of Immoral Use," destined to go down in history as the Comstock Act. The law barred the transportation of "any obscene, lewd, or lascivious book, pamphlet, picture, print, or other publication of vulgar and indecent character"—including material on contraception or abortion. The law didn't differentiate between pornographic photos and family planning pamphlets.* Comstock was now designated a "special agent" with the power to seize offending items.[92]

Comstock was highly suspicious of art, particularly of French derivation, or anything people were inclined to defend as such: For him, "art" was often a delivery mechanism for impure thoughts. He cared not a fig if Botticelli's *Birth of Venus* (1485) was considered "art": To him it was filth. "Art is not above morals," he wrote in an 1877 book, *Morals Versus Art*. "*Morals stand first.* Law ranks next as the defender of public morals. Art only comes in conflict with law when its tendency is obscene, lewd or indecent" (italics in original).

Comstock was especially concerned with literature's capacity to warp children's minds. He wrote his 1883 book, *Traps for the Young*, to "send a message to parents, so that they may avert from their homes a worse evil than yellow fever or small-pox." Literature's sole defensible purpose, he believed, was to ennoble the spirit. (He was hardly alone; the Victorian "genteel tradition," which held that literature was valuable only for moral improvement and the cultivation of etiquette, persisted well into the twentieth century.) Comstock hated the lurid half-dime novels and pulp magazines that "breed vulgarity, profanity, loose ideas of life, impurity of thought and deed. They render the imagination unclean, destroy domestic peace, desolate homes, cheapen women's virtue, and [turn readers] into foul-mouthed bullies, cheats, vagabonds, thieves, desperadoes, and libertines." His advice to parents: "Exterminate them."

....

* This distinction similarly eludes contemporary conservative and parents' rights organizations, which apparently cannot distinguish between books illustrating reproductive anatomy and "child porn."

Comstock clearly had exacting standards of appropriate reading material for children. He embraces a theory of mimesis, or imitation, that underlies many censorship efforts, before and since. "Do not forget that *lust breeds crime*," he wrote.[93] Reading about sex leads to temptation, which leads to premarital sex, shattered reputations, and lifelong dissolution. The line between book and behavior was direct.

But what motivated him, exactly? Why was he so obsessed with the moral purification of America's youth?

Many of Comstock's contemporaries suspected that his public crusade emerged from a private pathology. The lawyer Morris Ernst believed he was a chronic masturbator, as well as an "obvious psychopath." Ida Craddock, one of his targets, called him "a sex pervert; it is what physicians term a sadist." Comstock's biographers find evidence of "extreme self-loathing" in diary entries such as the following: "I debased myself in my own eyes today by my own weakness and sinfulness, and was strongly tempted today, and oh! I yealded instead of fleeing to the 'fountain' of all my strength. What sufferings I have undergone since ... each prayer or Hymn seemed to add to my misery."[94] Comstock appears to have devoted his professional life toward purifying others of anything that may have contributed to his own secret shame.*

Nevertheless, and despite the several attempts on his life (including once being stabbed in the face) by those

....

* Deep-seated anxiety about masturbation, like Comstock's, was widespread in nineteenth-century America. As the art history scholar Amy Werbel observes, self-appointed health experts like Sylvester Graham, inventor of the Graham cracker, warned that "self-pollution" could result in heart attacks, cancer, and death. "Hard beds, cold baths, and 'farinaceous' food were all advised," Werbel writes.

he had persecuted, Comstock was not one to be dissuaded, and carried on hounding, fining, and burning books right up until his death in 1915. One of his great enjoyments in life was breaking down the door of a suspected pornographer, gun drawn.[95] He measured his confiscated and destroyed literary matter by the ton. He claimed that his war on smut had resulted in 3,800 arrests and 2,881 convictions, resulting in over 565 years of jail time, and boasted that he'd driven 15 targets to suicide.[96]

* * *

IN 1915, AS Comstock's epoch of brutality was coming to an end, Sigmund Freud was writing about dreams. Specifically, he was searching for a metaphor to describe the way in which some internal, psychic authority seemed to edit our dreams, even as we sleep.

With the First World War raging to the east, Freud, based in Vienna, was living through a period of newspaper and postal censorship. Envelopes had to be left unsealed so that their contents could be read and expurgated as necessary; newspapers were riddled with gaps—white spaces where authorities had redacted information ("a pity, you feel, since no doubt it was the most interesting thing in the paper—the 'best bit,'" Freud wrote). He noted a strong parallel between these censored "blank spaces" and the gaps or ambiguities in our dreams, where a part of the mind has blurred out faces, muffled words, smudged details, or made euphemistic substitutions.

"Wherever there are gaps in the manifest dream, the dream-censorship is responsible for them," Freud wrote in a 1915 lecture, "The Censorship of Dreams." As Harvard historian Peter Galison contends, Freud would go further, "concluding that censorship could be called to account every time there was a dream element remembered 'especially faintly, indefinitely and doubtfully' among other, more familiar dream fragments."[97]

In Freud's theory of the unconscious, psychic censorship was responsible for blocking the dangerous impulses that we cannot bring ourselves to bear. (Like the censored bits of the newspaper, psychic censorship also draws attention to what it would repress.) If the desire to censor is ineradicable, then, if it seems to come naturally, that is because before it is externalized as social repression "censorship" also describes a psychic function—a repression of anti-social desires and fears that might otherwise disrupt our mental equilibrium.

Thinking back over the history of censorship, we see how the impulse to censor conforms to certain broad types. The paranoid censor silences others to consolidate power or safeguard his own ego; he censors to save himself. The righteous censor sincerely believes that if people are permitted to publish or speak as they please, the social order would collapse; he censors to save you, or your immortal soul. The perverse censor takes pleasure from his daily rubbings with the taboo, and thrills to exposing the "vices" of others. Beneath them all, if we believe Freud, lies a psychic operation in which some part of the mind censors the traumas, memories, and unacceptable desires that, if recognized, could impair our functioning in the world. Censorship, in this form, is the price of consciousness.

Of course, censorship's psychic motivations exist independently of its public justifications. Some of those aims may, incidentally, strike us as quite laudable, such as when

a group of anti-apartheid protesters destroyed Amster-
dam's South African Institute in 1984, or when English
suffragettes—who had already tried several forms of civil
disobedience including hunger strikes—firebombed a
public library in Birmingham, England, in 1914. These
activists saw their iconoclasm as justified by their eman-
cipatory aims: it's not as though they were harming or
killing human beings. And yet these righteous practi-
tioners of *libricide* join the Taliban in Afghanistan, Pol Pot
in Cambodia, Serbian nationalists under Slobodan
Milošević, and countless others who have burned libraries in pursuit of their dreams.

The habitual destruction of libraries throughout
human history—book banning in its rawest, most pri-
mordial form—points to another universal truth, which
is that books represent a threat to despotic power. As Lucien Polastron argues in *Books on Fire: The Destruction of
Libraries Throughout History*, libraries are constantly
threatened by a totalitarian need to erase the past:

> Why? Because, as the lawmakers of ancient China
> and the Nazis in Czechoslovakia decided, an edu-
> cated people cannot be governed; because the
> conquered peoples must change their history or
> their beliefs, like the Azteks; because only the illit-
> erate can save the world, a common theme of the
> millenarian preachers of every era; because the
> nature of a great collection of books is a threat to
> the new power, like Taoism in the eyes of the Mon-
> gols, or Shiism to the Sunnis, or the Reformation to
> traditional Catholicism.[98]

Backs to the wall, persecuted groups have burned their own libraries in order to save themselves. There is no ethnic cleansing without cultural erasure, and *libricide* is always handmaiden to genocide. As Polastron recognizes, every book burning is also an act of wishful thinking: "The book is the double of the man, and burning it is the equivalent of killing him." At its core, censorship is the primal expression of a desire to obliterate the Other, who displeases us by continuing to exist.

* * *

IF WE CAN imagine a spectrum of book banning, one end might consist of removing from a classroom a book that remains otherwise available. On the other end would be physical destruction of entire libraries. We may believe that such episodes belong to humanity's barbaric past. Sadly, as Rebecca Knuth demonstrates in *Burning Books and Leveling Libraries*, this is far from true.

By the time U.S. troops entered Iraq in March 2003, experts had warned what might become of the country's libraries and other cultural organizations. Indeed, in the buildup to the war, NGOs including UNESCO called upon the U.S. State Department to protect Iraq's fragile cultural infrastructure. The Blue Shield organization urged the U.S. to abide by the 1954 Hague Convention for the Protection of Cultural Property in the Event of an Armed Conflict. The American Library Association issued a statement, warning: "Cultural heritage is as important as oil. Libraries are a cornerstone of a democracy and are vital resources to the re-establishment of a civil society."[99]

These cautions went unheeded. After the fall of Saddam Hussein's forces in Baghdad, many of the country's libraries were ransacked. The University of Mosul, including its library and ancient manuscript collection, was pillaged by Iraqi citizens. In the end, "The entire collection of the National Museum, 170,000 precious artifacts of world history, including the earliest examples of writing, were reported as having been carried off or smashed," Knuth writes. "The National Archives and National Library were reported as twice victimized, first by looters and then by arsonists."[100]

Iraq's oil, deemed a strategic resource, was protected, while its cultural resources were stripped and ravaged. The U.S. military did not intervene to stop the looting and may have tacitly condoned it: U.S. Secretary of Defense Donald Rumsfeld openly mocked those who worried about the cultural rape of Iraq: "It's the same picture of some person walking out of some building with a vase," Rumsfeld said of media reports, "and you see it twenty times and you think, my goodness, were there that many vases? Is it possible that there were that many vases in the whole country?"[101]

Rumsfeld's response is not exceptional. It is, in the context of two millennia of *libricide*, utterly conventional. After all, why should we defend the cultural production of our ideological or military enemies, people with whom we may actually be at war? Why should we fight to preserve the ideas of people we may actively detest, those who may be committed to our own destruction? The answer lies in the liberal tradition of expressive freedom, to which we now turn.

3. Against Excremental Whiteness: Philosophical and Legal Foundations of Expressive Freedom

IN 1731, BENJAMIN Franklin founded America's first successful lending library. For a few years, Franklin had belonged to a group called the Junto—a debate club devoted to "mutual improvement"—who met in a tavern. But at a certain point, tired of being unable to consult their books for important facts and dates, they began meeting at the house of one of their members. Shortly thereafter, members decided to pool their books in a single room, such that each enjoyed "the advantage of using the books of all the other members, which would be nearly as beneficial as if each owned the whole," Franklin wrote in his *Autobiography*. He wondered about extending these advantages to the general public, and began selling subscriptions, for a modest fee (a requirement which was soon dropped), to a new institution. The idea took root, and the Library Company of Philadelphia, which Franklin called "the mother of all the North American subscription libraries," was born.

One of the keys to the Philadelphia Company's success was that its books weren't predominantly religious. To this point, the holdings of college and ecclesiastical libraries (non-lending libraries reserved for students) strongly reflected the interests of donors. The Philadelphia Company was perhaps the first institution to acquire books based on the interests of their readers (a commitment which remains one of the primary obligations of public libraries to this day). Its initial holdings were about 30% history, 20% (each) literature and science, 10% (each) philosophy and religion, and 10% miscellaneous. The library flourished "because it adopted a purchasing policy responsive to the needs of its intellectually alert, economically ambitious, but non-elite membership," the company's official history states.[102]

The formula worked. By 1800, more than forty lending libraries had sprung up in the United States.[103] In Franklin's view, "[T]hese libraries have improved the general conversation of the Americans, made the common tradesman and farmers as intelligent as most gentlemen from other countries, and perhaps have contributed in some degree to the stand so generally made throughout the colonies in defense of their privileges."[104] From their inception, then, libraries were associated with the defense of democracy. They bolstered expressive freedom and provided a bulwark against tyranny.

They were also understood to be engines of social mobility. Andrew Carnegie, the nineteenth-century industrialist who had amassed a fortune in the steel industry, attributed some of his success to an early benefactor who had once loaned him books—an experience which cemented Carnegie's belief in libraries as powerful incubators of self-improvement. His advice to aspiring tradespeople (mechanics, chemists, miners, etc.) was to gain advantage over their competition by reading everything the library had on their subject. Like Franklin, Carnegie also saw libraries as quintessentially democratizing.[105] "Free libraries maintained by the people are cradles of democracy," he said in dedicating the Washington, D.C., Public Library—one of the 2,509 free public libraries he helped to create around the world (including 125 in Canada). Carnegie built more libraries than anyone else in history, contributing to infrastructure that accelerated the spread of literacy, particularly in small communities.[106]

Since Carnegie's time, lending libraries have become enormously successful public institutions. Today, there are more public libraries (around 17,000) than Starbucks locations in the United States. Library books account for the majority of our reading: Canadian readers borrow 4.5 library books for every book they buy. The average library book is borrowed 8 times annually.[107] Digital borrowing has increased steadily: The Los Angeles Public Library system leads the way with 12 million annual online checkouts; OverDrive, a global digital e-book distributor for libraries and schools, reported 662 million borrowed titles in 2023.[108]

But our libraries are also under extraordinary pressure. The American Library Association reported more demands to ban books in 2023 than any year since it began compiling data about censorship. The atmosphere is tense: Librarians have faced harassment, bomb scares, and "bills threatening to criminally charge [them] or defund libraries altogether for making certain materials available on their shelves," according to Tracie D. Hall, ALA's former executive director.[109] Evangelicals and parental rights groups argue that libraries are riddled with LGBTQ+ "indoctrination" and works of "critical race theory," which burden children with guilt over slavery and genocide. Meanwhile, in their efforts to counter racism and bigotry, progressive educators in Ontario destroyed thousands of books which, they felt, reinforced systems of oppression. Both "sides" (which are really a single, pro-censorship consensus) construe books as sources of contamination from which children must be protected.

But if the answer to populist censorship is not progressive censorship, what alternative do we have? What is the correct response to those who would purge our libraries, trash the books they deem "offensive" (for whatever reason), and refill the shelves with books more suitable to their ideology? Where are those arguments to be found?

* * *

ONE OF THE foundational modern arguments for expressive freedom rose from the ashes of a failed marriage.

In June 1642, a thirty-four-year-old writer named John
Milton set off to Oxfordshire to collect on a debt. A man
called Richard Powell had fallen behind on his payments
to Milton's father, a financial broker and moneylender.
When Milton returned to London a month later, he was
married to Powell's seventeen-year-old daughter, Mary. At
least one Milton biographer called the marriage "a business transaction": Powell may have calculated that Milton
would be less likely to prosecute his own father-in-law for
defaulting on a loan.

Before long, however, the newlyweds were plagued
with communication issues. Milton may have been on his
way to becoming the greatest poet of the English language, but his teenage bride found him dull. The marriage
soon became unbearable to both.[110] Within months, Mary
Milton returned to Oxfordshire, and John Milton set to
work on a pamphlet, *Doctrine and Discipline of Divorce*, in
which he advocates for divorce in situations "whereof no
amends can be made, no cure, no ceasing but by divorce,
which like a divine touch in one moment heals all." Milton dedicated the tract to "The Parliament of England."

The Parliamentarians, however, weren't buying it.
They associated divorce with sexual libertines and scoun-
drels. "[A] wicked book is abroad and uncensored, though
deserving to be burnt, whose author has been so impudent
as to set his name to it and to dedicate it to yourselves,"
the Puritan Herbert Palmer preached in a sermon to parliament in 1643.[111] The Company of Stationers subsequently
flagged Milton's pamphlet as immoral.

Milton's divorce tract had arrived after the abolition of
the Court of Star Chamber in 1641, during what proved
to be a brief hiatus in England's censorship regime. In 1643,

Parliament passed a new Licensing Order, which reintro-
duced a requirement for pre-publication licensing, and
authorized the destruction of "offensive" books and the
flogging and imprisonment of delinquent writers and
publishers.[112] In short, by the summer of 1643, Milton had
attracted the scrutiny of state censors—which meant that
those censors had now attracted the scrutiny of John
Milton.

His next pamphlet, published in 1644, was *Areopagitica: A Speech of Mr. John Milton for the Liberty of Unlicenc'd
Printing to the Parlament of England. Areopagitica*—the
title referred to a speech delivered by the ancient Greek
orator Isocrates—laid the intellectual groundwork for
defending and justifying expressive freedom for subsequent generations.

Early modern authorities practised censorship for
many reasons, the most altruistic of which was a concern
for the souls of their subjects. Reading magical or heretical texts, it was assumed, could lead one spiritually astray.
Milton disputed this conventional wisdom. One of his
core arguments in *Areopagitica* is that "bad books" are not
simply sources of harm. Rather, to a "discreet and judicious Reader," Milton argues, bad books can "serve in many
respects to discover, to confute, to forewarn, and to illus-
trate."[113] Human beings were not intended to labour
under a "perpetual childhood of prescription," Milton
argues, but were rather entrusted "with the gift of reason
to be their own chooser." We should read "promiscu-
ously," he says. Without the ability to make our own
choices, our God-given reason is worthless.

But what about the frequent claim that books can promote evil ideas? If we took this argument seriously,

contends Milton, then the Bible—with its depictions of blasphemy, its elegant descriptions of carnal pleasures, and its ambiguous parables (capable of supporting unorthodox arguments)—would be among the first prohibited books. Banning books does not stem the transmission of wicked ideas: "Evil manners are as perfectly learnt without books a thousand other ways which cannot be stopt." Besides, ensuring the moral quality of books won't guarantee that readers will derive the right messages. A wise reader can gather wisdom from the most problematic text, while "a fool will be a fool with the best book, yea, or without book," he argues.

But Milton had a deeper point about the nature of good and evil. In attempting to curb evil by preventing the dissemination of "bad" books, we not only fail to stop the spread of evil, we also deprive readers the opportunity to acquaint themselves with the good. Milton arrives at a profound revelation:

> Good and evill we know in the field of this World grow up together almost inseparably; and the knowledge of good is so involv'd and interwoven with the knowledge of evill, and in so many cunning resemblances hardly to be discern'd ... It was from out the rinde of one apple tasted, that the knowledge of good and evill as two twins cleaving together leapt forth into the World. And perhaps this is that doom which Adam fell into of knowing good and evill, that is to say of knowing good by evill ... Assuredly we bring not innocence into the world, we bring impurity much rather: that which purifies us is triall, and triall is by what is contrary.

That vertue therefore which is but a youngling in the contemplation of evill, and knows not the utmost that vice promises to her followers, and rejects it, is but a blank virtue, not a pure; her whitenesse is but an excremental whitenesse.

Here is Milton's essential insight: Morality is relational. We recognize ethical categories not only by what they are, but also by what they are not. We know good *by* knowing evil. If you can imagine a world in which "evil" no longer exists—a world in which all forms of vice and sin have been vanquished, and people are unfailing in their ethical perfection—then you have also imagined a world in which "good" no longer exists, since "good" only ever made sense in contrast to evil. The beauty of Milton's insight is that it is entirely structural. It applies whether "good" means "Christian" or "anti-racist," and "bad" means "pornographic" or "Eurocentric." The good qualities become so through juxtaposition with their opposites.

Milton makes a similar point about virtue. There is nothing virtuous, he argues, about blind conformity. In fact, conformity for its own sake is a heresy of its own. True virtue is only possible when we acquaint ourselves with the full menu of evil and temptation, and then decline those seductions of our own free will. "I cannot praise a fugitive and cloister'd virtue, unexercis'd & unbreath'd, that never sallies out and sees her adversary, but slinks out of the race," he writes.

Yet "cloister'd virtue" is precisely what we enforce when we expunge our libraries of "bad books," however we define "bad." Censorship not only fails to prevent harm (as children will inevitably be exposed to the full range of human vice and depravity by other means), but becomes a new source of harm in itself by depriving students of the necessary conditions in which they could meaningfully discover their own virtue. Those behind the new censorship consensus forget this fundamental point: Those who are *forced* to be virtuous, aren't.

* * *

AREOPAGITICA CONTAINS MANY more arguments against censorship (including the point that books are never all good or all bad) and against censors themselves, who, if up to the task, would need to be uncommonly "studious, learned, and judicious," but who are in fact more likely to be "ignorant, imperious, and remisse, or basely pecuniary."* And then there's the separate question of who oversees the censors, who licenses the licensers, and so on.

Undergirding all of this is a vision of why people read. Milton provides an answer rooted in his own Protestant Christianity: We read to arrive at the truth. But censorship interferes with the process by which we can arrive at that truth. In fact, it is an insult to truth: "And though all the windes of doctrin were let loose to play upon the earth, so Truth be in the field, we do injuriously, by licencing and prohibiting to misdoubt her strength," he writes. "Let her and Falshood grapple; who ever knew Truth put to the wors, in a free and open encounter." Truth thrives

....

* While we shouldn't forget that Milton is officially concerned only with pre-publication licensing, scholars including John Rogers have argued that *Areopagitica's* soaring rhetoric and metaphor seem to push back against censorship writ large.

in conditions where it can confront falsehood. This idea forms the basis of the scientific method, the peer review process in academia, and empirical positivism: Truth is knowable by trial, and trial by what is contrary. Just as we would thwart the progress of scientists and mathematicians by denying them access to faulty formulas and disproven theories, so, too, do we impede our moral progress by erasing the errant pathways of wayward souls. Milton's deeper point is that, by "licencing and prohibiting," we not only deprive ourselves of the "untrue" examples we may have learned from, but we cut ourselves off from accessing the truth at all, which is the product of our internal judgment following moral trial.

Some argue that Milton's case for expressive freedom has, in our age of social media and rampant mis- and disinformation, outlived its utility. Think of the sheer volume of nonsense and false ideas sloshing through our social media troughs each day. What makes us so certain that misinformation on TikTok or X—concerns about pet-eating Haitian immigrants in Ohio, for instance—will be vanquished by truth?

This critique proceeds from a misunderstanding of how social media works. Milton believes that truth prevails over falsehood in a "free and open encounter," and many social media users seem to believe that this describes their experience. (Elon Musk has called Twitter the de facto public town square.) But the unseen algorithms that shape user experience on social platforms only give the appearance of freedom and openness. These algorithms are sets of digital instructions that constrain the field of information, tailoring it according to our usage patterns. An algorithmically defined social media feed is not in fact a "field" at all, but rather a voice. A 2024 Supreme Court decision, *Moody v. NetChoice*, states that "expressive activity includes presenting a curated compilation of speech originally created by others."[114] The algorithm speaks with its own biases. The virality of false ideas on social media points to the ways in which platforms prevent the "free and open" encounter Milton envisioned.

Milton's claim about truth prevailing over falsehood should not be taken as an absolutist defense of expressive freedom. Milton was not opposed to all forms of censorship—nor was he opposed to punishing the authors of particularly odious texts.* Rather, his argument is that texts shouldn't be suppressed prior to their publication because we need to judge them for ourselves. Truth, for Milton, cannot be imposed from above. The man who believes things "only because his Pastor sayes so" is what Milton calls a "heretick in the truth": he is a heretic even if he holds the "right" views.

What are the consequences of Milton's position in our time? Confronted with proliferating online mis- and disinformation, some contend that we can no longer afford the radical freedom that Milton construes as necessary for the individual discovery of truth. These powerful new platforms, they claim, require governments or corporations to exert centralized or private control over speech to ensure that citizens have access to truthful information. (In making this claim, they echo the pro-censorship arguments that early modern authorities had made about the disruptive media of their own time, the printing press.)

....

* Milton would not extend expressive freedom to Roman Catholics, for instance—a conventional view in a society in which the pope was commonly held to be the Antichrist.

Doubtless, misinformation can cause deadly harm. In 2019, for instance, one peer-reviewed public health study "linked increases in measles cases with the proliferation of global anti-vaccine campaigns."[115] But the distinction between truth and misinformation is not always clear-cut. In 2021, after U.S. President Biden accused social media platforms of "killing people" with COVID-19 misinformation, Facebook censored "lab leak" posts which claimed that the virus had originated at the Wuhan Institute of Technology. In a subsequent statement, Mark Zuckerberg acknowledged that his team had caved to government pressure in removing the posts.[116] By 2023, however, FBI Director Christopher Wray said that his agency had concluded that the virus "most likely" came from a "Chinese government–controlled lab."[117] The case had the unfortunate consequence of seeming to vindicate the view that governments and corporations had been lying to their citizens about the origins of the virus. This was just one example of how top-down efforts to police expression and force a particular truth upon the public can easily backfire, undermining citizens' confidence not only in the particular "truth" in question, but also the very institutions and authorities who insist that they must control speech for our own good.

Even in cases where we can clearly distinguish between factual and fake news, the impact of disinformation on democratic outcomes may be exaggerated. One American study of the 2016 election, for instance, found that while disinformation was rife—some 30 million false pro-Trump stories and 8 million false pro-Clinton stories were shared on Facebook alone—the overall effect of this fake news "would have changed vote shares by an amount on the order of hundredths of a percentage point…much smaller than Trump's margin of victory." The researchers found that fake news tends to reinforce narratives that are already held by voters.[118] Therefore, while disinformation can certainly bring destructive impacts in some cases—increasing vaccine hesitancy, for instance—the "cure" of censorship is often worse than the proverbial disease. In fact, as the cultural historian Jacob Mchangama argues, our exaggerated concerns over the ability of our fellow citizens to succumb to misinformation may represent a form of "elite panic" that has been used to justify censorship throughout history. "Liberal democracies must come to terms with the fact that in the [digital realm] one cannot effectively shield citizens and institutions from hostile propaganda, hateful content, or disinformation without compromising the egalitarian and liberal values of democracy as such," Mchangama argues. Such top-down censorship "is as unlikely to instill a spirit of trust, understanding, and compromise as it is to succeed in filtering away all undesirable information."[119]

Milton, of course, was a religious man, writing for religious times. Final "Truth," as he conceived of it, would become apparent only with the resurrection of Jesus Christ. Until then, we have to make do with the truth that emerged from the process of our own judgments. Unquestioned belief in what a pastor, politician, or content moderator tells us is but an "heretickal" truth. We need to read, think, and decide for ourselves.

Milton's arguments reveal the moral naïveté of book banning. In attempting to prescribe public morality by purging "immoral" books, book banners insult their own ideals by presuming they can't withstand an open conflict with their opposites. More devastatingly, by reducing libraries to scenes of "excremental whiteness," or enforced virtue, the new censorship consensus robs readers of their own opportunity to discover truth in opposition to falsehood. That is, in expunging the "harmful" texts (whether due to stereotypes, slurs, or LGBTQ+ content), they prevent readers from thinking through their own responses, and thus defining their own values, ethics, and truth. The censors would reduce education to the recitation of dogma; in so doing, they turn their own truths into heresies to be overcome.

* * *

IN 1858, A fifty-two-year-old English civil servant and his wife toured the south of France, scouting locations for their retirement. Not long into the trip, however, the woman, Harriet Taylor, came down with a rasping cough. By the time they arrived in Avignon, she was suffering from full-blown lung congestion. The man wrote a panicked letter calling for their doctor and used the new telegraph machine to summon their daughter at once. Neither arrived in time.[120]

John Stuart Mill sat with his dead wife for a full day in their Avignon hotel room, his life unspooling. Mill loved Taylor with an unusual ferocity: the monument he commissioned in her memory would be fashioned from the Carrara marble used for Michelangelo's *David*. "It is doubtful if I shall ever be fit for anything public or private again," Mill wrote after her death. "The spring of my life is broken." Weeks later, he sent his latest manuscript to his publisher, dedicated to "the memory of her who was the inspirer, and in part the author, of all that is best in my writings." That manuscript was *On Liberty*, another foundational document in the history of expressive freedom.[121]

Mill's subject in *On Liberty* was the "nature and limits of the power which can be legitimately exercised by society over the individual." This was not exactly fresh philosophical terrain, as Mill recognized. But he sensed a universal tendency to "stretch unduly the powers of society over the individual"—a seemingly natural disposition among rulers and fellow citizens toward domination. Each generation had to refortify individual sovereignty against the encroachment of social control, and Mill proposed a principle for doing so: "The only purpose for which power can be rightfully exercised over any member of a civilized community, against his will, is to prevent harm to others. His own good, either physical or moral, is not a sufficient warrant. He cannot rightfully be compelled to do or forbear because it will be better for him to do so, because it will make him happier, because, in the opinions of others, to do so would be wise, or even right." This idea came to be known as Mill's "harm principle," and it would remain a staple in philosophy classrooms for generations.[122]

Mill believed in the sovereignty of the individual. Human flourishing requires the freedom to choose our own values and goals, the freedom to decide what kind of person we want to be, how we want to spend our one precious life. We must be left alone to pursue our aims, even if others "think our conduct foolish, perverse, or wrong." Our society should aspire not toward conformity, but to diversity: Mill advocates for "different experiments of living," for giving full latitude to "varieties of character."

The "worth of different modes of life should be proved practically," he writes. Diversity is good not only in itself, but also because it is educative. Other people should be free to live their own lives, partly so that we can learn how to live ours.

Above all, Mill's understanding of the good life depends upon comprehensive freedom of consciousness and opinion on every subject, including the liberty to express those opinions: There's no point in holding an opinion that can't be shared. The freedom to read and to publish was fundamental to the kind of liberty that Mill saw as constitutive of human flourishing. He recognizes that most of us likely agree with this freedom in principle—except perhaps in cases where dangerous opinions threatened the very stability of society itself, in which case a democratic government, "entirely at one with the people" might impose restrictions. But even in this case, Mill argues—even if the government is perfectly aligned with its constituents—censorship is indefensible. "I deny the right of the people to exercise such coercion, either by themselves or by their government," Mill writes. He continues:

> The power itself is illegitimate. The best government has no more title to it than the worst. It is noxious, or more noxious, when exerted in accordance with public opinion, than when in opposition to it. If all mankind minus one, were of one opinion, and only one person were of the contrary opinion, mankind would be no more justified in silencing that one person, than he, if he had the power, would be justified in silencing mankind.

Those behind the new censorship consensus should be made to confront this point. It doesn't matter if you, as self-appointed arbiter of social conscience, *think* you are correct; it doesn't matter if you really *are* correct, or if you are acting with the blessing of the majority. (Indeed, it is worse if you are.) The power *itself* is illegitimate. Removing library books amounts to social coercion, in clear violation of Mill's harm principle.

We may think Mill is hyperventilating when he says that humanity is no more justified in silencing one person than that person would be in silencing the rest of humanity. But Mill is not exaggerating; he means it literally, and it's important to understand why. In a scenario where all of humanity silenced one dissenter, the victim is not only the dissenter, but all of humanity. Censorship harms not only the person who is silenced, but also the exponentially greater number of people who could never test their own views against his. (This is true even if the censored person is in fact wrong, and the majority is right.) "To suppress free speech is a double wrong," as Frederick Douglass argued in 1860. "It violates the rights of the hearer as well as those of the speaker."[123]

But what could be wrong with purging our libraries of books that are harmful to children, assuming we could agree upon what those materials are? Would we not be correct in censoring books that are dangerous to learners?

In Mill's terms, those who make such arguments have confused *their* certainty for *absolute* certainty. History is awash with cautionary tales of authorities who projected their personal certainty onto the world, with calamitous results. So certain were Catholic authorities that the sun orbited the earth, they attempted to obliterate the writings of Copernicus and Galileo. So certain were twentieth-century scientists of eugenics and the racial hierarchy, they sterilized tens of thousands of Canadians and Americans to control "undesirable populations." So certain were nine-teenth- and twentieth-century educators in the superiority of their methods and the purity of their intentions, they created a residential school system for Indigenous students that would become synonymous with cultural genocide.

Novels once written off as obviously obscene are now hailed as timeless masterpieces. Artists once attacked as "degenerate" now find their work in museums and anthologies, while their persecutors have been sharply rebuked by history.

Are we smarter, or more ethical, than the humans who arrived at these judgments? How can we avoid repeating their devastating mistakes? Our only mechanism for testing the validity of our ideas is open disputation, which entails a modicum of intellectual humility—an awareness that we may, in fact, be wrong. The only solution is to preserve space for others to contradict and disprove our claims: "On no other terms can a being with human faculties have any rational assurance of being right," Mill argues. However certain we are of any opinion, "if it is not fully, frequently, and fearlessly discussed, it will be held as a dead dogma, not a living truth."

Censorship obstructs our one pathway to truth. It turns each of us into an ill-informed tyrant, surrounded by terrified sycophants who will tell us only what we want to hear, thus depriving us of the ability to discern the truth of anything. Censorship turns our own knowledge about the world into superstition.

Those who would purify our school libraries do not understand this, or think they know better. They are endowed with their absolute certainty. They presume to know not only what your child should read, but also how they will read it. They know that *Flamer*, a queer coming-of-age memoir, is a work of sexual titillation. It does not occur to them that *Flamer* could inspire compassion, empathy, or self-acceptance. There is perhaps no better antidote to corrosive certainty than diverse reading, but this is an experience the book banners categorically deny for themselves, for your children, and for their own. These contemporary Comstocks think they know your child's mind. They would not only make our decisions for us, but also deprive us of the opportunity to judge for ourselves.

Who would you trust to do your reading for you? Which administrator or bureaucrat would you appoint as your own censor—to decide what information you can't access, which ideas you shouldn't know? Who is qualified to determine that a book, an author, or an entire field of inquiry should cease to be? The correct answer is: no one. Only those who have abandoned the sovereignty of their own minds and souls could answer otherwise.

* * *

LIKE MILTON, MILL is not a free speech absolutist. Mill thought that speech should be curtailed when it would result in harm to others. "An opinion that corn-dealers are starvers of the poor, or that private property is robbery, ought to be unmolested when simply circulated through the press," he writes, "but may justly incur punishment when delivered orally to an excited mob assembled before the house of a corn-dealer."* Speech should be regulated only when it might reasonably be expected to cause harm to others—and it is clear from this example that "harm" means direct physical harm. The problem with Mill's mob isn't that it might make the corn dealer feel unsafe, but that it might tear him limb from limb.

Mill's harm principle obliges us to think carefully about certain library books. Take, for example, *Hit Man: A Technical Manual for Independent Contractors*, published by Paladin Press in 1983. As the title makes clear, *Hit Man* is a how-to guide for those interested in a new career as an assassin. Chapters tackle mental and physical preparation; sourcing equipment; finding employment (what to charge, who to avoid); surveillance tips, and other practical advice ("if the mark has a bad heart, the mere presence of a venomous snake in his bed or mailbox might bring about an immediate heart attack").

Ten years after its publication, a man named James Perry used *Hit Man* for its intended purpose, killing a woman, her disabled eight-year-old son, and his nurse. Survivors sued Paladin Press for aiding and abetting murder. Paladin didn't dispute the nature of the book—it was, after all, a detailed guide on how to get away with murder. Instead, they argued—successfully, as it turned out—that the book only "advocates or teaches murder," and does not "incite or encourage" murder, and was thus protected under the First Amendment. A subsequent rul-

....

* This famous example has taken on new relevance in the wake of the January 6, 2021, storming of the U.S. Capitol. Words that are acceptable in one context can be physically dangerous when delivered to an excited mob.

ing by the Fourth Circuit Court of Appeals reversed the decision, finding that preparing people for "imminent lawless action" is not, in fact, protected under the First Amendment. The plaintiffs ultimately settled with Paladin's insurance company.[124]

Mill's harm principle might lead us to conclude that *Hit Man* has no defensible place on library shelves. Still, even in the seemingly straightforward case of a killer's manual, legal minds have wrangled over the distinction between "teaching" and "inciting" harm. The U.S. legal threshold for incitement turns out to be high indeed. Paladin agreed to stop selling *Hit Man* as part of a settlement, although its full text remains available to anyone with an internet connection, and has been for years.

* * *

SOME ACCOUNTS OF free speech give pride of place to the First Amendment, passed in 1791, which states that Congress shall "make no law" that would abridge "the freedom of speech, or of the press." In practise, the First Amendment provided no such assurance—not in 1798, when John Adams published the Sedition Act, making it a federal crime to "write, print, utter or publish" with "intent to defame" the president or the U.S. government[125]—and not in 1918, when Woodrow Wilson's Congress passed its own Sedition Act, criminalizing "disloyal, profane, scurrilous, or abusive language" about the United States and its military draft in the First World War.[126]

The First Amendment coexisted with vigorous campaigns of state-sponsored book banning throughout the nineteenth and twentieth centuries. That censorship involved post office confiscation, customs seizure, civil and criminal prosecution, and police arrests.[127] Some of the world's great literature was put on trial, including James Joyce's 1922 novel, *Ulysses*. Particularly concerning were the following lines:

> And then a rocket sprang and bang shot blind blank and O! then the Roman candle burst and it was like a sigh of O! and everyone cried O! O! in raptures and it gushed out of it a stream of rain gold hair threads and they shed and ah! they were all greeny dewy stars falling with golden, O so lovely, O, soft, sweet, soft!

Supposedly, the above description of Leopold Bloom pleasuring himself ended up in the hands of a young woman, whose parents subscribed to *The Little Review*—a magazine that excerpted this fateful chapter of *Ulysses*. The outraged parents complained to the DA, and a judge declared that *Ulysses* was the "work of a disordered mind." A subsequent letter to *The Little Review* reveals the moral temperament of the age: "I think this is the most damnable slush and filth that ever polluted paper in print ... There are no words I know to describe, even vaguely, how disgusted I am; not with the mire of his effusion but with all those whose minds are so putrid that they dare allow such muck and sewage of the human mind to besmirch the world by repeating it—and in print, through which medium it may reach many young minds. Oh my God, the horror of it!"[128]

In 1932, Random House decided to test the legality of the ban on *Ulysses*. They imported an edition published in France, hoping it would be seized at the border; when it wasn't, a Random House lawyer returned it to Customs for another look. A public trial for *Ulysses* would (the publisher hoped) generate a scandal and stimulate sales. Finally, in the fall of 1933, the United States Southern District Court of New York heard *United States v. One Book Called* Ulysses, which was destined to become a landmark obscenity case.

Arguments began on November 25. The publisher's lawyers wanted to prove that *Ulysses* was written for "edification and delight." They submitted hundreds of testimonies from reviewers, scholars, and authors (including F. Scott Fitzgerald) to establish that *Ulysses* was a literary "classic." ("James Joyce's position in literature is almost as important as that of Einstein in science," asserted critic Malcolm Cowley. "Preventing American authors from reading him is about as stupid as it would be to place an embargo on the theory of relativity.") *Ulysses* was an intricate aesthetic achievement, they argued—the very opposite of commercial titillation or obscenity.

But how was "obscenity" to be defined? For the answer, courts routinely turned to an 1868 English case which formulated the famous Hicklin Test. According to *R. v Hicklin*, a publication was obscene if it, in whole or in part, elicited a tendency to "deprave or corrupt those whose minds are open to such immoral influences, and into whose hands a publication of this sort may fall."

The "in whole or in part" stipulation was important. The publisher's lawyers argued that the Hicklin Test didn't apply, because prurient readers wouldn't survive even a few pages of Joyce's sinuous, allusive prose. Moreover, they argued, obscenity was a living standard; *Ulysses* had to be judged according to the morality of the time, not of fifty or even ten years before. The novel's acceptance by a community of scholars and professionals proved that it couldn't be obscene. The government argued, by contrast, that obscenity hinged upon the response of an "average reader...[and that] on these grounds there are ample reasons to consider *Ulysses* an obscene book."

On December 6, 1933, Judge Woolsey pronounced his verdict. He believed that Joyce intended to represent the interior consciousness of his characters, which required a certain sexual candour. The sexual subject matter was inherent to Joyce's technical innovation. Woolsey had conducted the world's smallest focus group, asking two friends if *Ulysses* had "aroused them to lust," and they assured him it had not. Woolsey concluded: "I am quite aware that owing to some of its scenes *Ulysses* is a rather strong draught to ask some sensitive, though normal, persons to take. But my considered opinion, after long reflection, is that whilst in many places the effect of *Ulysses* on the reader is undoubtedly somewhat emetic, nowhere does it tend to be aphrodisiac. *Ulysses* may, therefore, be admitted into the United States."[129]

Judge Woolsey's decision helped liberalize obscenity law in some specific ways: He evaluated the publication as a whole, not just in part. He considered its standing among experts. He thought about what the book was trying to achieve. He assumed a mature readership.

Adherents of today's censorship consensus would have us unlearn all these lessons. Their checklists focus on parts of a book, rather than the entire work. They suppress the book's overall intention, ignore its standing among experts, and assume a highly immature, pliable readership.

* * *

POSTWAR WRITERS ENJOYED expanded freedom to explore sexual themes, but change wasn't instantaneous. In 1945, the Massachusetts Supreme Court upheld a ban on the sale of Lillian Smith's novel *Strange Fruit*, finding in it an imminent "danger of corrupting the public mind." When, in 1953, ACLU lawyers attempted to make a free-speech case for Henry Miller's *Tropic of Capricorn* and *Tropic of Cancer*, federal courts declined to hear it.

A milestone case (and the end of the Hicklin Test) arrived in 1957's *Roth v. United States* in which bookseller Samuel Roth was charged with violating federal obscenity statutes for purveying the magazines *American Aphrodite* ("A Quarterly for the Fancy-Free") and *Good Times: A Review of the World of Pleasure*. While Roth was ultimately convicted—the Court's decision, authored by Justice William J. Brennan, found that obscenity was not protected by the First Amendment—Brennan's decision narrowed "obscenity" to mean sexual material "appealing to prurient interest." "Prurient interest" was still debatable, but this refinement allowed that "sex and obscenity are not synonymous," which broadened the scope of expressive freedom. (The distinction between sex and obscenity is one that pro-censorship forces are still seeking to elide.)[130]

Meanwhile, in a separate 1957 decision finding that Allen Ginsberg's poem *Howl* was not obscene, Judge Clayton Horn asked: "Would there be any freedom of press or speech if one must reduce his vocabulary to vapid innocuous euphemism? An author should be real in treating his subject and be allowed to express his thoughts and ideas in his own words."

In 1964, the Supreme Court reversed Florida's ban on *The Tropic of Cancer* on account of its literary value (which couldn't "vary with state lines"). The same rationale would liberate Burroughs's *Naked Lunch* in 1966. And 1973's *Miller v. California* reaffirmed that erotic literature was constitutionally protected (in contrast to obscene materials, which were not) and established yet a new obscenity test—specifically, "a) whether 'the average person, applying contemporary community standards' would find that the work, taken as a whole, appeals to the prurient interest ... b) whether the work depicts or describes, in a patently offensive way, sexual conduct specifically defined by the applicable state law; and c) whether the work, taken as a whole, lacks serious literary, artistic, political, or scientific value."[131]

While municipal and state governments had been expanding their censorship capacities throughout the 1950s, censorship boards began to wither in the 1960s. The fate of the Georgia Literature Committee is representative. Founded in 1953, the committee's remit was to aid prosecuting attorneys "in the administering of laws of the state regarding obscene literature." It accrued more power as the decade wore on; by 1958, it had authority to issue injunctions and to stop the distribution of books (which it used on titles including *Turbulent Daughters* and *Rambling Maids*). The committee reviewed 427 complaints in 1964. By 1967, it reviewed just 22 complaints. And in 1973, the committee was formally dissolved by Georgia governor Jimmy Carter.[132]

What happened? There were the succession of Supreme and Superior Court decisions finding, variously, that obscenity was a federal issue, that the entire work had to lack artistic merit, and that obscenity was a living standard, and standards change. Cultural norms were evolving over the 1960s, and the courts' decisions reflected that shift as much as they reinforced it. By 1972, the year of *The Last Tango in Paris* and *Deep Throat*, pulp novels like *Turbulent Daughters* and *Rambling Maids* no longer struck fear into the hearts of many Americans. Compared to the immediacy of filmic depictions of hardcore pornography, Joyce's image of a bursting candle in *Ulysses* seems positively genteel.

By the dawn of the 1970s, mainstream writers could depict sex in ways their literary forebears would not have dared. Philip Roth's Alexander Portnoy was free to fuck the liver that his family would eat for dinner. In 1976, the Canadian novelist Marian Engel published *Bear*, featuring a relationship between the protagonist and the eponymous mammal. (Actual dialogue: "Eat me, bear.") The book suffered no legal consequences. To the contrary, it was awarded the Governor General's Literary Award, selected by a jury that included Mordecai Richler, Margaret Laurence, and Alice Munro.

Even as the culture was becoming more permissive, however, "obscenity" remained a contested category. With the proliferation of the queer press in the 1970s and '80s, prosecutors increasingly turned their attention to gay and lesbian writers, publishers, and booksellers—and "obscenity" became their weapon of choice.[133]

* * *

THE BODY POLITIC was a path-breaking platform for gay liberation. The periodical, published monthly in Toronto from 1971 to 1987, both covered and engaged in queer advocacy. It organized protests over bathhouse raids, drew attention to the AIDS epidemic before mainstream news outlets did, and helped uncover the extent of Nazi persecution of gays and lesbians during the Holocaust.

But on December 30, 1977, the Toronto police's morality squad raided *The Body Politic*'s offices, carting off twelve boxes of subscription lists, records of advertising and classified ads, corporate documents, and more. The eventual charges, focusing on an article entitled "Men Loving Boys Loving Men," included "possession of obscene material for distribution" and "use of the mails for the purpose of transmitting indecent, immoral or scurrilous materials."

Prominent figures, including mayor John Sewell and journalist June Callwood, publicly sided with *The Body Politic*, while civil liberties lawyer Clayton Ruby undertook its defence. The Crown prosecutor's witnesses included a clinical psychologist who believed that homosexuality was a sexual disorder, and a local reverend known for organizing anti-gay protests and pressuring school boards to ban Salinger's *The Catcher in the Rye*, Margaret Laurence's *The Diviners*, and other books.

In the end, Justice Sydney Harris found that the Crown failed to prove that *The Body Politic* breached community standards with "Men Loving Boys," although his judgment could hardly be mistaken for approval: "Shocking and offensive to the community it may be, disgusting and even upsetting as well, even distasteful, sickening, unsettling or appalling; but I find that indecent as a whole it is not."

Still, the police kept up their campaign against *The Body Politic*. The raids and criminal trials would continue for years—largely redounding in favour of the publication, if also at the steep financial and psychological costs of the editorial members who were subject to criminal proceedings.[134]

* * *

AMONG THE MOST enduring tools of literary censorship are national customs laws. Canada prohibited the import of publications deemed "immoral and indecent" from the time of the nation's founding; a new Customs Act replaced those words with "obscenity" in 1985.[135] By 1990—a moment in which Canada had one openly gay MP—customs inspectors were detaining for evaluation 75% of the books and magazines shipped to Glad Day Bookshop in Toronto, L'Androgyne in Montreal, and Little Sisters in Vancouver. Most bookstores were never subject to seizures of this sort, but for those specializing in gay and lesbian literature it was increasingly routine.

Thousands of books and magazines were confiscated. Those that met the threshold of "obscenity" were summarily destroyed; those that didn't would arrive in damaged condition, months late, or not at all. Customs inspectors detained erotica, literature (by Ginsberg, Burroughs, Isherwood, and others), biography, even scholarly work. Because anal penetration was deemed obscene, many representations of male homosexual sex were inherently problematic.

Courts across the Anglosphere had long struggled to define obscenity. Perhaps the most famous formulation arrived in 1964, with U.S. Justice Potter Stewart's folksy assertion, "I know it when I see it." In the mid-1980s, the Canada Border Services Agency tried a more comprehensive approach with Memorandum D9-1-1, Policy on the Classification of Obscene Material. Its appendices provide a taxonomy of "obscenity indicators" which are almost comically precise:

Depictions and / or descriptions of:

(a) Sex with degradation or dehumanization, if the risk of harm is substantial, e.g.

(i) actual or implied urination, defecation or vomit onto or into another person, and / or the ingestion of someone else's urine, feces or vomit, with a sexual purpose, excluding consensual urination onto or into another person or the consensual ingestion of someone else's urine.

In practise, D9-1-1 became another cudgel with which to attack queer bookstores. This routine harassment sometimes boiled over into legal prosecution, as was the case when police seized a copy of *Bad Attitude* (a self-described "lesbian sex magazine") from Toronto's Glad Day Bookshop in 1992. The trial focused on a fictional story featuring what the store's owner described as a "play rape scene"; the legal question was whether the sex it depicted was "degrading or dehumanizing." The defence argued that it fell within community standards, submitting (among other things) Madonna's hit book *Sex*, which featured images of the iconic singer bound and nearly naked, with a knife at her throat. The case attracted media attention from the *Los Angeles Times* and elsewhere; the *New York Times* wondered if "serious" books were now at risk from Canada's "morals police."*

Glad Day was guilty as charged. "This material flashes every light and blows every whistle of obscenity," the judge decreed. "Enjoyable sex after subordination by bondage and physical abuse at the hands of a total stranger."[136] In this case, Canada's obscenity law—which had been sharpened with an eye to protecting women from the harmful effects of pornography—had succeeded in criminalizing queer expression.

The judge insisted that sexual orientation was not a factor in his decision. But the unavoidable conclusion, in the words of the legal scholar Brenda Cossman, was that the "test for obscenity was subject to discriminatory interpretation against sexual minorities."[137]

How, then, to minimize or counter that discrimination? Some have proposed prohibiting anti-LGBTQ+ expression as a way of addressing the enduring problems of homophobia and bigotry. In 2023, for instance, LGBTQ+ activists called for the banning of Abigail Shrier's *Irreversible Damage: The Transgender Craze Seducing Our Daughters*. As Chase Strangio, an attorney with the American Civil Liberties Union, tweeted: "Abigail Shrier's book is a dangerous polemic with a goal of making people not trans . . .

---

* By 1993, the question about whether "serious" books were in danger in Canada was answered, when one customs officer named Corrine M. Honey decided that graduate students at Trent University could not study the Marguerite Duras novella *The Man Sitting in the Corridor*. Ms. Honey's official reason for seizing thirty copies of the book was "sex with violence." The shipment was eventually released upon appeal.

Also stopping the circulation of this book and these ideas is 100% a hill I will die on."[138] When public libraries in Nova Scotia refused to remove Shrier's book, Halifax Pride announced that it would no longer hold events in any public library location. Some wonder why the government can't simply step in and ban Shrier's book.

The long history of LGBTQ+ legal persecution shows why this impulse is misguided. The campaigns against queer presses, writers, and booksellers reveal the historical failure of authorities to overcome their own biases in adjudicating questions of obscenity. Those biases in our legal system must be addressed. But we must also recognize that laws expanding expressive freedom have contributed to social and legal victories for sexual minorities, while laws restricting and criminalizing speech have consistently reinforced their subjugation.

Those invested in safeguarding LGBTQ+ rights should be especially concerned with upholding a robust regime of expressive freedom against those who would use "obscenity" as a means of legalizing their own bigotry.

* * *

THIS LEGAL HISTORY reveals something else, which is how contingent, how fragile these norms really are. We sometimes think of "the law" as a rock-solid and immutable edifice. But the history of "obscenity" reveals how laws are always shaped by arguments and interpretations of individual people at specific moments in time. For fifty years, First Amendment jurisprudence has provided guardrails against much censorship and widened the scope of expressive freedom. Instead of national or statewide bans, today's book banners have therefore devoted their energies toward libraries and school boards. At the same time, the fall of *Roe v. Wade* provided a harrowing reminder that laws are always open to revision. Some state legislatures are already working to revivify censorship functions that had atrophied in the postwar decades. Georgia's Senate Bill 154 is one of several legislative efforts that could open librarians to prosecution under obscenity laws.[139]

To repeat: Obscenity is based on community standards, and standards change. In the postwar decades, law and culture tacked in the direction of greater expressive freedom, but there is no guarantee that future standards won't veer in the opposite direction. With Donald Trump's 2024 election win, and the likelihood of two more Trump-appointed Supreme Court Justices, conservative dominance of the Court is assured for decades to come. Legal censorship may be poised for a generational comeback.

At the very minimum, given that community standards are open to debate, we must brace ourselves for the coming legal and cultural contest over expressive freedom. The fight against censorship is never over; it must be renewed by each generation. Liberal societies must reaffirm our commitments to the free exchange of ideas. In doing so, we find a powerful source of arguments in the liberal tradition. That lineage, which includes Locke, Spinoza, Montesquieu, and countless others, finds particular inspiration in the writings of John Milton and John Stuart Mill—thinkers who articulate how the freedom to read and write is constitutive of human liberty.

4. Words That Wound: Intellectual Challenges to Expressive Freedom

WHEN EDUCATORS IN Ontario's Peel District School Board (PDSB) purged thousands of library books in 2023 as part of an "equity based weeding process," they did so with certain assumptions in mind. Chief among them, as spelled out in an internal training manual, is that the region of Peel "operates in white supremacist structures where socially constructed hierarches of different [*sic*] privilege some and marginalize others." Part of their solution involves transforming the school library—rife with books that "reinforced colonial ideologies that are inherently racist, classist, heteronormative, and ableist"—into a Library Learning Commons (LLC), which affirms a student's right to "resources that mirror their lived experiences."[140]

The purges were necessary, the board believes, to center the "lived experiences" of students, which means their experience as racialized and gendered subjects. It was all part of a broader shift "away from educators being the experts, toward the truth that the wealth and the beauty and knowledge rests in the community," as the manual explained. In explicitly devaluing the expertise of librarians and other educators, progressive book banners echo the logic of parents' rights activists in the U.S. who similarly question the authority of experts and insist that school libraries mirror the experiences and values of the home. Regardless, the LLC's new purpose is not to encourage literacy or research skills, but to "promote anti-racism, inclusivity, and critical consciousness."[141]

The PDSB manual specified that, to remain culturally relevant, books were to be retained for no more than fifteen years from their publication date. If enacted, this policy would ensure that all copies of Malala Yousafzai's *I Am Malala: The Girl Who Stood Up for Education* will be pulled from Peel schools by 2028. Juno Dawson's *This Book Is Gay* will follow in 2029, Angie Thomas's *The Hate U Give* in 2032, and Ibram X. Kendi's *How to Be an Anti-racist* in 2034. Peel students would never discover books by James Baldwin, Maxine Hong Kingston, or Maya Angelou in their libraries, as all of their books were first published more than fifteen years ago and therefore not, according to the PDSB, culturally relevant.*

* The manual doesn't specify whether new editions of old books would be evaluated according to their original publication date or the publication date of the most recent edition. The manual's "Guidelines for the Weeding of Fiction Resources" section states that the "retention period based on publication date" for general fiction is ten to fifteen years. Due to the manual's consistent emphasis on "the currency and relevance of the collection," and references to books written within students' lifetimes, my understand-

This unwavering emphasis on children's lived experience—high school libraries would exclude anything
published before students were born—aspires to
near-perfect historical presentism and near-zero cultural
continuity: were the fifteen-year retention period permanently enacted, a child born next year will read none
of the books that a current ninth grader has read to date;
parents will have no literary experiences in common
with their children. Entire historical episodes, such as
the internment of Japanese Canadians, will likely vanish
from the shelves; some historically significant texts,
including Anne Frank's *Diary*, are already gone. PDSB's
presentism assumes, unrealistically, that publishers can
fill the historical gaps left by weeding older books; since
Canada has less domestic publishing capacity than the
U.S., Canadian school libraries will become increasingly
dependent upon American content. Of course, new
books on historical subjects will not necessarily be better
than older ones, and may not be written or published. In
all likelihood, students interested in history will be left
to YouTube or whatever they can find online—which is,
after all, where they spend much of their "lived
experience."

If there was one species of book PDSB educators were
told to regard with particular skepticism, it was the
so-called classics. "The category of 'Classics' typically
consists of Euro-centric texts that were penned long
before students' birth dates, and may not reflect the lived
experiences of students," the manual states. "In doing this

---

ing is that the LLC is to consist of texts that were *first* published fifteen
years ago or later. Including reprints of classic texts would contradict their
insistence on currency.

work, we need to be acutely aware of the fact that nothing is neutral."

These ideas have an intellectual history. That history has roots in the thinking of Brazilian Marxist Paulo Freire, who saw education as intrinsically political, and in that of Frantz Fanon, the French Afro-Caribbean philosopher of decolonization. Above all, they proceed from the thesis that language can be a form of violence—that words can wound. And that idea began to coalesce at Harvard University in 1981.

According to the scholar Kimberlé Williams Crenshaw, critical race theory (CRT) began with a 1981 student boycott at Harvard stemming from the departure of Derrick Bell. Bell, a pioneering legal scholar of "racial realism"—which posited racism as an ineradicable and determining force within American society—had recently left Harvard for a deanship at the University of Oregon. When Harvard failed to replace Bell with another professor of colour, Crenshaw, along with graduate student Mari J. Matsuda and others, organized an alternative course in which prominent Black academics delivered weekly guest lectures based on Bell's book *Race, Racism and American Law*. Two of those guest lecturers, Richard Delgado and Charles R. Lawrence III, would, along with Crenshaw and Matsuda, write a book of their own: *Words That Wound: Critical Race Theory, Assaultive Speech, and the First Amendment* (1993).

Taking their cues from Bell, the authors of *Words That Wound* presented racism as endemic to American institutions, including the law and higher education. If their intellectual contribution could be boiled down to a single concept, a single word—one that would influence a generation of thinkers and reverberate far beyond the academy—that word was *systemic*. It was misleading to think of racist "incidents," caused by flawed individuals— your proverbial bigoted uncle. It was wrong to imagine a few racist fish in a sea full of decent fish. Racism was inextricable from the sea itself. Racism was profoundly imbricated with the very institutions and principles we normally thought of as safeguarding freedom. Federalism, privacy, "traditional values," including the value of free expression—all were "vessels for racial subordination."

In the context of the law, racism wasn't a product of imperfect jurists, but rather a characteristic ingrained in foundational concepts, including "neutrality, objectivity, color blindness, and meritocracy." In any social arena in which systemic inequalities of opportunity led to an inequality of outcome, be it in health care, education, criminal justice, income, or political representation, racism was the notable contributing factor.

On a methodological level, critical race theory privileged the "experiential knowledge" and "lived experience" of survivors of racism, which meant elevating the subjective experience of people of colour over "objective" or "neutral" principles (such as colour blindness under the law). Critical race scholars regarded these neutral principles with suspicion, as potentially compromised by unacknowledged biases. In civil rights doctrine, "areas of law ostensibly designed to advance the cause of racial equality often benefit powerful whites more than those who are racially oppressed," they write in the introduction to *Words That Wound*. The most insidious racists are not necessarily the purveyors of "gutter" hate speech— the ones who will insult you to your face. More ominous are the "polite and polished colleagues," who deploy "codes," including "merit, rigor, standards, qualifications, and excellence" as part of their "backlash" against "women and people of colour." One of the most telling features of "these colleagues" is that they "mourn the passing of an era when we 'all' read the 'great books.'"*

The ultimate goal of the critical race theorists was the elimination of racial oppression, which, they acknowledged, was impossible in the current liberal-capitalist order. Therefore, they measured progress "by a yardstick that looks to fundamental social transformation."[142]

* * *

THE ESSAYS COLLECTED in *Words That Wound* examine specific incidents of assaultive speech, including racist slurs, humiliating images and insults, and derogatory comments. They argue for an expanded regime of speech regulation in professional contexts (such as university campuses) and in society at large (through reforms to criminal and civil law). "When victimized by racist language, victims must be able to threaten and institute legal action, thereby relieving the sense of helplessness that leads to psychological harm," Richard Delgado argued in the title essay.[143]

By protecting racist speech, Delgado argued, the law is essentially privileging the white bigot's freedom to use

....

* Which isn't in itself a condemnation of the "great books." In other words, we can gladly bid "good riddance" to an era in which "we" (upper-class white men) all read the same "great books," while also recognizing that it was not the books that were the era's problem, but rather the racism that contributes to unequal outcomes in education, incarceration, income and wealth, property ownership, health and lifespan. The problem is that "great books" came to be seen as one of the "codes" (along with merit, rigour, etc.) of backlash, rather than sources of power for the dismantling of racism.

racist insults over racialized people's right "to lead their lives free from attacks on their dignity." Sure, victims are legally entitled to the liberal panacea of "more speech," including, presumably, some choice epithets of their own, in responding to the original racist insult. But this fails to consider both the uneven power relations and the psychologically debilitating quality of the racist blow received.

Indeed, the psychological violence of racist speech is the driving rationale for regulation. Matsuda asserts that "victims of vicious hate propaganda experience physiological symptoms and emotional distress ranging from fear in the gut to rapid pulse rate and difficulty breathing, nightmares, post-traumatic stress disorder, hypertension, psychosis and suicide." Delgado writes, "American Blacks have higher blood pressure levels and higher morbidity and mortality rates from hypertension, hypertensive disease, and stroke than do white counterparts."[144] Free speech liberals, following Mill's harm principle, want to separate words and deeds, such that only "incitement to harm" should run afoul of the law. The critical race theorists, by contrast, insist that racial epithets incite harm—direct, physical harm—in themselves. These words trigger an immediate and lasting "psychic destruction" that manifests in the body. Whether they "led to" violence was beside the point, because they *are* violence. Hence the need for stronger regulation.

Recent research has further underscored the bodily effects of social injustice. Arline Geronimus, a public health scholar, uses the term "weathering" to describe biopsychosocial chronic stressors—including "environmental toxins, suffering indignities and interpersonal racism"—which disproportionally affect marginalized people, especially Black women. In *Weathering: The Extraordinary Stress of Ordinary Life in an Unjust Society*, Geronimus finds that toxic stress reinforces "persistent, entrenched racial inequalities in health" and contributes to excess mortality in marginalized populations."[145]

* * *

CRITICAL RACE THEORY changed the way we talk about race, not only in academic disciplines, but in the broader culture. No informed person today would deny that racism is "systemic" in the sense that redlining and other segregationist policies were programmatic and entailed significant intergenerational economic harm. The case for reparations has been proved. Critical race theory was also helpful in provoking legal scholars to re-examine the trade-offs between individual harms caused by racist abuse and fidelity to principles—ideas which were in danger of becoming "dead dogma." Many of them did.*

It is also easy to see, from our vantage point, how progressive educators appropriated and broadened a set of CRT assumptions which have made equity-based book banning seem morally necessary. One of those elements was the primacy of experiential knowledge—that which is gained, according to the authors of *Words That Wound*, "from critical reflection on the lived experience of racism." Another is the assumption that words can cause psychological if not physiological harm—which was

* See, for instance, Henry Louis Gates Jr., Anthony P. Griffin, Donald E. Lively, Robert C. Post, William B. Rubenstein, and Nadine Strossen, *Speaking of Race, Speaking of Sex: Hate Speech, Civil Rights, and Civil Liberties* (New York: NYU Press, 1994).

accompanied by a corresponding rejection of the traditional liberal distinction between words and conduct.
The library thus became a scene of literal violence.

True, the authors of *Words That Wound* focused on the
most heinous examples of assaultive speech. But it is also
true that the N-word, today considered the most wounding of words, appears in many books that may yet lurk on
a library's shelves, including *The Adventures of Huckleberry Finn*, *Of Mice and Men*, and *Heart of Darkness*.

Encountering racist speech in the context of an historical narrative is not necessarily equivalent to being on the
receiving end of verbal "vicious hate propaganda"
directed at you personally. But those behind the PDSB
book purge weren't interested in differences between spoken and written words, or the contextual factors framing
how language is received. And having accepted the prem-
ise that racist words (and stereotypical images) are
violence, they went further, construing the absence of
identity-affirming words as another source of harm: thus,
the PDSB manual lists "lack of representation" alongside
"slurs" and "racism" as sources of oppression. Where the
critical race scholars expressed skepticism toward "dom-
inant legal claims of neutrality, objectivity, color
blindness, and meritocracy," progressive educators
applied that skepticism toward neutrality onto library
books with their equity toolkits. *Where the Wild Things
Are*, *The Hobbit*, *Animal Farm*—any book that isn't identity-
affirming and responsive to lived experience is part of the
problem. (Remember: There is no neutral ground.) As
the PDSB manual instructed teacher librarians: "Holding
onto personal biases such as 'But I love / loved that book'
promotes practices that prioritize teacher-centered

approaches." The love of literature is just another bias to overcome, another way in which oppressive power rein-scribes itself.

The authors of *Words That Wound* proposed the regulation of assaultive speech, and PDSB applied that lesson, too, to the library. While one can imagine a range of regrettable responses—including warning labels on books, requirements for parental permission, separate sections for "harmful" books, and the like (all of which are being implemented in various U.S. jurisdictions)—PDSB administrators leapt straight to the expurgation of "harmful" books. Some will wonder why we couldn't simply add *more* books to the library—more books which celebrate BIPOC, LGBTQ+, or other marginalized identities. From the critical race perspective, this call for "more books" is akin to U.S. Supreme Court Justice Louis Brandeis's call for "more speech," which they rejected on its face. "More speech" is liberal doublespeak which would excuse the continued existence of harmful representations—an apology for systemic racism, as well as an example of it. Or, as the PDSB manual puts it: "We cannot layer new inclusive and exciting resources alongside racist, oppressive and colonial resources!"[146]

* * *

THE PDSB'S ATTEMPTS to import CRT-inspired ideas into their libraries raises a number of thorny problems, including the question of who decides whether a particular word, book, or image is wounding. The critical race scholars were clear that people with lived experience of racism were the only ones who could adjudicate this question.

Where else would the offence register than in the subjective experience of the offended party? Yet the Ontario School Library Association (OSLA) pointedly excludes subjective offence as grounds for challenging library books: "It is very important," the organizations states, "that the role of the reconsideration procedure is not to assess the resource in question according to the values of the challenger." Instead, concerns are evaluated according to the relevant selection guidelines.[147] The OSLA concedes the impossibility of issuing self-authorizing veto power to every library user on the basis of their lived experience.

Others have questioned the parameters of "wounding" words. In an essay responding to *Words That Wound*, Harvard professor Henry Louis Gates Jr. argues that the category of wounding words "includes but is scarcely exhausted by racist speech. Nor could we maintain that racist insults, which tend to be generic, are necessarily more wounding than an insult tailor-made to hurt someone: being jeered at for your acne, or obesity, may be far more hurtful than being jeered at for your race or religion."[148]

If our goal is to eliminate words that "wound," the category of "wounding" words may end up being far more capacious than originally intended, especially in heterogeneous, pluralistic societies like the United States and Canada—and especially if, per the critical race scholars, it is up to the victims to define what hurts. Mormons, Muslims, Jews, LGBTQ+, disabled and neurodivergent students, and others may declare themselves to be the victims of violent words, and neither the original critical race scholars nor the progressive educators provide us with satisfactory frameworks for balancing what may end up being competing harms. Should libraries affirm the identities of religious fundamentalists who believe that the presence of LGBTQ+ literature amounts to harmful indoctrination? What happens when socially conservative parents decide that their own lived experiences, cultural norms, and community values must be "mirrored" in school libraries? There is no way out of this bind. Educators must either admit that certain lived experiences count for more than others or divest from identity affirmation as the sole rationale for reading and literacy.

After *Words That Wound* was published, some First Amendment scholars asked why minorities would entrust institutions with expansive powers to determine the limits of permissible speech. Nadine Strossen, then president of the ACLU, argued that the attention to speech "may well divert our attention from the causes of racism to its symptoms." Banning library books does little to address inequalities in wealth, incarceration, infant mortality, and so on. Moreover, treating free expression as part of systemic racism also risked obscuring "how effectively it has advanced racial equality," Strossen argues.[149] Gates, meanwhile, observes that such well-intentioned censorship powers often rebound unexpectedly. "During the year in which [the University of] Michigan's speech code was enforced," he observes, "more than twenty blacks were charged—by whites—with racist speech . . . not a single instance of racist speech by whites was punished."[150] In a more recent survey of hate speech laws, Timothy Garton Ash finds "no correlation between the presence of extensive hate speech laws on the statute books and lower levels of abusively expressed prejudice about human difference."[151]

Over the last few years, Republicans have caricatured CRT as a "monstrous evil," as Pat Robertson called it.[152] In 2020, the conservative activist Christopher Rufo told Tucker Carlson that CRT was "an existential threat to the United States" and called for President Trump to "immediately issue an executive order to stamp out this divisive, pseudoscientific ideology at its root."[153] Over a three-month stretch in 2021, Fox News mentioned CRT nearly 1,300 times.[154] This version of CRT bore little resemblance to the writings of Richard Delgado and Mari Matsuda, whose work was never mentioned.* Rather, it was a populist fever-dream, a scapegoat for anti-Americanism—the disagreeable Other who must be silenced. Republican state houses set out to ban teaching CRT concepts from schools, while the right-wing media frenzy over white guilt energized the parental rights censorship groups.

While right-wing book banners were going after the *1619 Project* and other CRT works, progressive educators in Canada were appropriating CRT-adjacent ideas—that words wound, that claims to neutrality and expressive freedom work to naturalize existing hierarchies, that the defence of "great books" is a species of racist apologetics— to legitimate a book purge of their own. Attempts to ban CRT from classrooms are attempts to undermine liberal democracy itself, not only because liberalism's legitimacy hinges upon its ability to confront the historical injustices and the failures of its institutions, but also because CRT's critiques of those institutions were justified. Where the conservative and progressive adherents of today's censor-

....

* Nor did it seriously engage with later CRT scholarship, which by now encompasses a vast body of valuable and largely pro-democratic work (although I do not presume comprehensive knowledge of this methodology as a whole).

ship consensus err is in presuming that we can censor our way out of history and its entanglements. We can and must reckon with our national failures without sacrificing expressive freedom as an ideal. The solutions involve a rearticulation and reaffirmation of those ideals, not purging our libraries of every book that may cause harm.

Some words can wound, and direct, assaultive speech has no place in our educational institutions. But we insult students' intelligence by invoking "harm" as a blanket category, one that might cover anything from PTSD-style trauma to mild discomfort. We further demean students by implying—as progressive book banning cannot fail to imply—that the experience of being victimized by assaultive speech is equivalent to discovering an epithet in a nineteenth-century novel. What we desperately need is a new educational vocabulary for distinguishing wounding words from necessarily discomfiting historical inheritances. Students must be taught that language is a social construct to be historicized and interrogated, not mythologized. Rather than inculcating moral hubris, educators should sustain ambiguity, nuance, sympathy, and curiosity as they guide students through the multi-faceted complexities of history. The education theorist Paulo Freire was right to criticize what he called the "banking model" of education, which treated students as passive receptacles of information. Yet this is precisely how children are construed by those who insist that books must be removed from shelves before they can fill students with their harmful contents.

* * *

LET ME OFFER a final reflection on the notion that defending "great books" can be a code for racist backlash. When Matsuda et al. made this argument in 1993, they were rightly criticizing professors who refused to include women and non-European writings in their courses. Such reactionaries still exist, albeit mostly on the margins of a profession that has embraced diversity as a prime imperative. The PDSB progressives went further, arguing that the presence of what they call "classic" literature—with its Eurocentric and colonialist values, and its irrelevance to students' lived experience—is potentially harmful to learners, and has no place in today's school library.

Many Black and racialized readers have, of course, found that classic literature speaks directly to their lived experience. In *The Message*, Ta-Nehisi Coates describes how, as a high school student, he recognized in *Macbeth* something of the same wounded striving that he saw in the streets of Baltimore and in the lyrics of rap artists like Kool G Rap. *Macbeth* pulled him across centuries, Coates writes, and "through words I understood that my Baltimore was not damned, that what I saw in the eyes of the boys there, what I heard in the music, was in fact something old, something ineffable, which marked all of humanity, stretching from Stratford upon Avon to the Streets."[155]

Why are some educators unwilling to recognize the powerful ways in which classic literature resonates with the lives of minority students? "Too often, teachers have a preconceived notion of our students' identities and of what should feel true to them," writes Roosevelt Montás, long-time director of Columbia University's Center for the Core Curriculum. Montás, who immigrated from a rural village in the Dominican Republic when he was eleven years old and unable to speak English, found a volume of Plato's *Dialogues* in a garbage pile. This chance discovery changed the course of his life.

"It was not my identity as a Dominican immigrant that Socrates affirmed, but something more fundamental," Montás writes. An "identity that felt true to my deepest self." Socrates's ideas "were not just about something that had happened a long time ago to an old man in ancient Greece. They had meaning for me right where I was and just as I was."[156]

Those who would purge our school libraries of "classic" literature claim to be "centering students," when in fact they are centering their own theories of education and reducing access for those who are less privileged. Their beliefs about what students should read emerge not from the children's own interests, but from identitarian categories that have been naturalized in the process of the teachers' professionalization. Educators risk reinscribing an old and insidious form of racism, implying, through acts of censorship, that racialized students needn't concern themselves with the likes of Shakespeare or Socrates—that these works aren't really "for" them. Historically, this prohibition has been accompanied by a strong push in the direction of vocational training.*

The progressive critique of "classic" literature as "Eurocentric" misses the mark. Classic texts now include literature from all over the world. But even works from

---

* As W. E. B. Du Bois observed in *The Souls of Black Folk* (1903): "We daily hear that an education that encourages aspiration, that sets the loftiest of ideals and seeks as an end culture and character rather than bread-winning, is the privilege of white men." Du Bois firmly rejected this. "I sit with Shakespeare," he wrote. "I move arm in arm with Balzac and Dumas...I summon Aristotle and Aurelius and what soul I will."

the European Renaissance, for instance, are always being reinterpreted in new, and often anti-colonial, ways. A recent selection of books on Shakespeare includes *Latinx Shakespeares: Staging U.S. Intracultural Theater*; *Teaching Social Justice Through Shakespeare: Why Renaissance Literature Matters Now*; *White People in Shakespeare: Essays on Race, Culture and the Elite*, and *Shakespeare / Sex: Contemporary Readings in Gender and Sexuality*.

Classic texts continue to evolve with the interpretations and critical perspectives of new readers. Part of what makes these works "classic" is that they reward critical reinterpretation over time and empower the imagination of subsequent generations. Rare is it to find a "canonical" book that straightforwardly advocates for a specific way of life; more frequently, they are "the acid which reveals the outlines of abusive power."[157] Intentionally depriving disadvantaged students the opportunity to engage with classical literature only compounds their immiseration: the very opposite of equity.

A Postmodern Postscript

IF YOUR EDUCATION included university English courses in the 1990s or 2000s, chances are you encountered a host of thinkers that are described, not always accurately, as "postmodern." I'm thinking of mid-to-late-twentieth-century philosophers like Jacques Derrida, Roland Barthes, Michel Foucault, and their many interpreters and acolytes. These thinkers could be thrilling to read, because they refused to take anything for granted. Sex, power, the very nature of language and words—all of it was fair game. Among those thinkers was an English and legal scholar named Stanley Fish, and one of the ideas that he refused to take for granted was free speech. Fish's arguments in his 1994 book *There's No Such Thing as Free Speech ...And It's a Good Thing, Too* must rank among the most serious philosophical challenges to expressive freedom. While those arguments may ultimately legitimate too much censorship and lead to negative social consequences, they warrant serious attention for the uncompromising pressure they place on the boilerplate arguments for free speech.

Fish forces us to confront an important truth, which is that every society contends with speech that it will not tolerate. Even John Milton, author of those stirring words about letting truth and falsehood collide in open conflict, was not prepared to extend those freedoms to "Popery, and open superstition, which as it extirpats all religions and civill supremacies, so it self should be extirpate ... that also which is impious of evil absolutely either against faith or maners no law can possibly permit, that intends not to unlaw itself."

What explains Milton's rabid anti-Catholicism (beyond the anti-Catholic prejudices of his milieu, and the parliamentary audience of *Areopagitica*)? For Milton, Catholicism cannot be tolerated because it won't tolerate the Protestantism which grounded Milton's truth—the stable foundation against which all other judgments could be formed. The law cannot permit ideas that would "unlaw" the law itself. Fish's point here is that every society has this category of intolerable speech, "intolerable" because it is profoundly inimical to the continuation of that society, and that "free" expression emerges against this background of the unsayable. As Fish puts it:

> When the pinch comes (and sooner or later it will always come) and the institution (be it church, state, or university) is confronted by behavior subversive of its core rationale, it will respond by declaring "of course we never meant to tolerate _____, that we condemn," not because an exception to a general freedom has suddenly and contradictorily been announced, but because the freedom has never been general and has always been understood against the background of an originary exclusion that gives it meaning.

Fish's argument is well taken and clarifies for us why free speech "absolutism" is untenable. He mentions the case of Jim Keegstra, the Alberta high school teacher who was convicted of hate speech and lost his professional accreditation for teaching that the Holocaust did not occur. The free speech absolutist might reply, "Of course we never meant to tolerate teaching Holocaust denialism to school children, that we condemn." Or they will say that teaching is a unique case, subject to profession-specific rules, like rules against insider trading, or false advertising, or disclosing state secrets, which are carved out from the larger domain of free speech. All of this only strengthens, rather than rebuts, Fish's point: "speech" emerges against conditions of unfreedom constituted by language and law—conditions which are repressed by those who talk about "free speech."* Since speech is always regulated, he believes, it's up to us to ensure that the line is drawn where we want it drawn.

This idea isn't as complicated as it may sound. Anyone who has read William Golding's *Lord of the Flies* will remember the importance of the "conch." In their rudimentary "town hall" meetings, the stranded boys initially agree to speak only while holding the shell, which is a talisman for civilization. The conch's real superpower, in this context, is to impose silence on others: Free speech can only become free in a context where others will listen,† (As Fish argues, "Free expression could only be a primary value if what you are valuing is the right to make noise.") When the conch loses its power to silence, the boys' germinal civilization shatters, and they devolve into savagery. (*Lord of the Flies*, one of the most challenged books of the 1990s for its violence and crude language according to the American Library Association, is now banned in progressive jurisdictions due to Golding's use of the N-word.)

Fish's larger point is that speech is never "just" speech—it is only meaningful insofar as it is "for" this or that. Rather than defending "free speech," Fish urges us to recognize that the "core rationale" of our institutions is not the production of speech for its own sake but rather the reproduction of the fundamental values that further that core rationale itself. And when speech acts are

....

* In other words, all speech unfolds against a backdrop of what is already silenced or unsayable. Fish's point is about the constitution of language itself, but we might simply think about it in terms of our internal social "filters" that stop us from spewing every thought that "freely" enters our minds. It's impossible to imagine a functional society without those filters.

† Strictly speaking, "listening" is less important than the condition of silence (in the sense that one needn't *listen* to John Cage's "4'33" for the formal existence of the silence).

contrary to that core rationale, they ought to be regulated. As Fish states:

> When someone observes, as someone surely will,
> that antiharassment codes chill speech, one could
> reply that since speech only becomes intelligible
> against the background of what isn't being said,
> the background of what has already been silenced,
> the only question is the political one of which
> speech is going to be chilled, and, all things con-
> sidered, it seems a good thing to chill speech like
> "n*****," "c***," "k***," and "f*****." And if
> someone then says, "But what happened to free-
> speech principles?" one could say [that] free-speech
> principles don't exist except as a component in a
> bad argument in which such principles are
> invoked to mask motives that would not with-
> stand close scrutiny.*

Fish's argument sounds sweeping and polemical, and
in a sense it is. But what he's calling for is perhaps no
more radical than Section 1 of the Canadian Charter of
Rights and Freedoms. Section 2 establishes the "freedom
of thought, belief, opinion and expression, including the
freedom of the press." But Section 1 had already established that these freedoms are "subject only to such
reasonable limits prescribed by law as can be demonstrably justified in a free and democratic society." Where Fish
argues that free speech can't be an end in itself, it must be
for something, the framers of the Canadian Charter have

---

* Fish does not censor the epithets in his text—a minor but notable indica-
tion of how norms have changed since the 1990s.

already told us what that something is: the furtherance of a free and democratic society.

Yet as Henry Louis Gates Jr. points out, and as Fish knows, evaluating speech according to its goals simply "defers the question" about where to draw the line, rather than helping us draw it. This approach is not without risk, even in cases where the "aims" of speech may be perfectly justifiable. Again, take the Canadian Charter, with its stipulation that speech can only be regulated if "demonstrably justified in a free and democratic society."

Let's imagine that a new populist government decided to ban the teaching of critical race theory on the grounds that such a ban is "demonstrably justified in a free and democratic society." To support its case, a conservative think tank adduces scholarly evidence to demonstrate CRT's incompatibility with democracy. Such an effort might produce Henry Louise Gates Jr.'s contention that, "Like so much sweepingly utopian rhetoric, they [the critical race thinkers] would also signal a regime so heavily policed as to be incompatible with democracy." Or they could turn to Yale legal scholar Robert Post, for whom a "necessary consequence" of CRT's calls for legal regulation "will be the wholesale abandonment of all principles of freedom of expression."[158] Or they could point to certain lines from the critical race theorists themselves—their call for "fundamental social transformation," for instance—to "demonstrably justify" the banning of CRT in Canadian schools.

But what if we would argue (as I do) that critical race theory should *not* be banned, that teachers ought to be free to teach material that might make some students uncomfortable (even if some found it to be undemocratic)? We are left with the argument that even books and ideas that aren't compatible with democracy and freedom, which may even be openly *hostile* to democracy and freedom, should still be permissible, and may even be beneficial within a liberal democracy—for precisely the reasons that Milton, Mill, and the other liberal thinkers have outlined over the centuries: because strong intellectual critique allows us to rethink our own beliefs from the ground up; because the prohibition of counter-arguments would reduce our beliefs to "dead dogma"; because we are not infallible, and ideas we are convinced are wrong could contain aspects of truth; because citizens must have the right to choose, and a forced choice is no choice at all. In other words, we are left with a pile of arguments in support of a principle that, for Fish, doesn't exist.

* * *

STANLEY FISH PUTS his finger directly on the sore point for free speech liberals: How can we claim to be "for" expressive freedom while simultaneously being against Holocaust denialism or (actual) pornography in schools? Put simply, Fish argues that this reveals that we are never simply "for" free speech (which doesn't exist), and that speech must therefore be evaluated in the context of its goals. As he says, "Speech in and of itself cannot be a value and is only worth worrying about if it is in the service of something with which it cannot be identical." And if you were to argue that a Floridian book banner or autocratic dictator might embrace Fish's logic in its pursuit of censorship—free speech doesn't exist and so we examine speech's goals; we find our enemies' goals to be contrary to our social vision and therefore ban their speech—Fish would say that this is what Western democracies are already doing, even if they don't admit it, and that it is always up to us as citizens to fight for the kind of speech we want to protect.

Fish's claim is that if we want to debate whether pornography or the teaching of CRT ought to be banned in schools, we should have those arguments on their merits, rather than referring to free speech principles, which would perpetuate a "bad argument in which such principles are invoked to mask motives that would not withstand close scrutiny." This, it seems to me, is half right, and gets at the core of our disagreement with Fish. It is true that every society and organization—church, state, and social media platform—must draw lines separating acceptable from unacceptable expression. Few of us would choose to spend time on a social media platform that circulated snuff films, child porn, or unlimited bot-generated spam. Fish is also right that our decisions about contested or objectionable speech must be made on the merits of the specific speech itself—which is to say that context is everything. As J. S. Mill argued, it's one thing to criticize a corn dealer in the newspaper, and another to lead an angry mob to his house. The same words can mean different things in different circumstances. Societies need to be able to make fine-grained distinctions based not only on the specific speech act, but also on the situation in which it occurs. We can, and should, prohibit the teaching of junk science and Holocaust denialism in elementary schools, while permitting its expression in other contexts, including books that are freely available in the library.* But in order to understand *why* we should permit the expression of odious ideas, we must appeal to the very free speech principles that Fish has rejected. We must permit objectionable speech not for what the speech itself is "for," or in service of, but because of what it allows *us* to do, which is to subject our own assumptions to "trial by what is contrary."

In short, Fish believes that our prohibitions against speech in certain contexts proves the non-existence of the principle of free speech, full stop. There are philosophical and pragmatic issues with this position. First, the philosophical objection: even if we were to grant Fish his central point, it's not clear why the non-existence of free-speech principles should weaken our commitment to them. Our lives are structured around fictions that do not exist and yet exert an objective force in reality. Some fictitious entities, like rumours or disinformation, point to their own lack of factual truth even as they shape existing reality. Scholars have called these entities *objective fictions*, which not only blur the lines between things that objectively exist and those that do not, "but draw our attention to the antagonistic, *contradictory* character of objective reality itself as something objective."[159] Free speech may not exist as anything but an objective fiction, but that doesn't mean that attacking and undermining it won't lead to objectively greater conditions of unfreedom.

Which leads us to the more pragmatic point. Freedom of expression refers not only to a principle; it is also a

---

* The Toronto Public Library was right to stock Robert F. Kennedy Jr.'s *The Real Anthony Fauci*; the reasons for doing so are even more urgent now, after his pending appointment as HHS Secretary. We need to know what and how he thinks to effectively respond and protect our institutions.

human right, codified in Article 19 of the United Nations Universal Declaration of Human Rights, which affirms the "freedom to hold opinions without interference and to seek, receive and impart information and ideas through any media and regardless of frontiers." I don't think Fish intends to trivialize or assert the non-existence of this right, but nonetheless "free speech doesn't exist" isn't a heartwarming slogan for the 339 writers currently jailed in 33 countries around the world.[160] Fish isn't making a pro-censorship argument, but he does undermine the anti-censorship position by insisting upon the non-existence of its underlying principle.

Fish's argument was partly a product of its moment, the early 1990s. These were years in which liberal democracy seemed to have emerged as the uncontested and most perfect form of human governance—years in which we had arrived at the "end of history," in Francis Fukuyama's phrase. Liberal principles, including free speech, had been necessary to escape the violently authoritarian, non-democratic regimes in the seventeenth and eighteenth centuries. But by the post-authoritarian 1990s they may have started to feel like articles of faith, perhaps even dead dogmas in and of themselves.[161] Accordingly, scholars of the '90s theorized power in more comprehensive and counterintuitive terms: Censorship wasn't just something a government did to repress its citizens, it was inscribed into the disciplinary norms that created us as human subjects. For the theorist Michael Holquist, for instance, "To be for or against censorship as such is to assume a freedom no one has. Censorship is."

Stanley Fish is far from an activist.[*] It may be unfair to think about the consequences of Fish's ideas in practical, social, political, and cultural struggles; his work is accountable only to advancing his discipline. If academic freedom means anything, it means freedom to explore ideas independently of social or political accountability. But those of us engaged in public argument would be well advised to evaluate his ideas according to the standards that Fish himself advocated: that is, by thinking about the larger purposes for which his speech is in service. "You assert, in short, because you give a damn, not about the assertion," he claimed, "but about what your assertion is about."

And now that the forces of authoritarianism and totalitarianism are again ascendent, as liberal democracy and its freedoms are again imperilled, we are finding that our principles are hard to live without. When the book banners arrive at the school of your children or grandchildren, or where you yourself teach, when you take to the podium, you will not proclaim that "free speech does not exist," or that censorship "is." Fish's arguments will remain important in the context of advancing the academic discipline, which is ultimately what they are about, but those who give a damn about combatting censorship will find more inspiration in Milton, Mill, Frederick Douglass, and in the free-speech principles that, Fish is convinced, do not exist.

....

[*] See *Save the World on Your Own Time*, in which he argues that academics ought to "advance bodies of scholarship" and keep their politics out of the classroom.

5. Future-proofing Our Freedom to Read

EACH DAY, IT seems, brings news of another book banning controversy. In Utah, conservative activists have targeted Little Free Libraries, arguing that owners should face prosecution if they distribute "obscene" literature.[162] In Texas, members of parental rights groups have reportedly begun approaching schoolteachers directly, providing them with lists of books which, they insist, must be removed from classroom shelves.[163] Censorship is rising in prisons, where it goes largely unopposed: One report found that Florida's carceral system bans some twenty thousand titles for nudity, violence, or reasons never provided. Louisiana prisons banned a book on Leonardo da Vinci; Texas banned a visual Spanish-English dictionary.[164] Given this rising tide of censorship, some public libraries have pre-emptively declared themselves "book sanctuaries." Hoboken, New Jersey, has identified itself as a "Book Sanctuary City."

Harder to quantify, yet impossible to ignore, is the "soft censorship" that occurs when titles are excluded or limited to avoid bans. Dr. Seema Yasmin reports that her children's book *The ABCs of Queer History* was soft-banned when a big-box retailer cancelled a large order prior to publication. "What I expected was more of, 'A parent in Dallas County has said they don't want the book taught in their school.' I did not expect a huge corporation to order and then rescind a 10,000-copy order," Yasmin said.[165]

After decades of postwar liberalization, pro-censorship arguments are resurgent in state legislatures and court-rooms. In Llano County, Texas, officials recently argued that library collections constitute government speech and are thus not open to First Amendment challenges. The government has "no constitutional obligation to include a particular book within a library's collection," lawyers claim, and is not required to "facilitate anyone's efforts to obtain a particular book"—essentially making a case for the library as purveyor of only state-approved content. Library advocates warn that the court's acceptance of this argument would "upend everything that a public library is supposed to be." The decision from Texas's Fifth Circuit, which has been called "the most conservative court in the land," is expected within months.[166]

Meanwhile, conservative lawmakers have rediscovered an old tool: the 1873 Comstock Act, which was never repealed. The Alliance Defending Freedom, a Christian advocacy group, recently argued before the U.S. Supreme Court that the act prohibits the mailing of mifepristone, an abortion pill. Indeed, the law's sweeping prohibition of mailing "obscene" and "lewd" material means that "provoc-ative art pieces, anything that vibrates or lubricates, IVF,

Viagra, sex-education materials, abortion medications, and all things LGBTQ" could be targets, according to Planned Parenthood. "Companies like FedEx and UPS could transform from neutral carriers into moral gatekeepers, forced to police the contents of their packages."[167]

Project 2025, the conservative Heritage Foundation's nine-hundred-page wish list for Donald Trump's second presidency, promises to supercharge book banning: "Pornography, manifested today in the omnipresent propagation of transgender ideology and sexualization of children … has no claim to First Amendment protection," the document claims. "Its purveyors are child predators and misogynistic exploiters of women … the people who produce and distribute it should be imprisoned. Educators and public librarians who produce and distribute it should be classed as registered sex offenders."[168] Regardless of the degree to which Donald Trump will implement these Heritage Foundation priorities, the censorious impulse woven into Project 2025 isn't going anywhere, and will seek to effect policy wherever it can.

Fighting book bans is now a part of the business model for large publishing companies, who are increasingly involved in First Amendment litigation to protect the rights of readers and authors. Results have been mixed. In Iowa, for instance, a U.S. District Court sided with a coalition of publishers, teachers, and authors who sued the state over an expansive 2023 education law that resulted in 3,400 books being pulled from schools. An Appeals judge subsequently dismissed the injunction, allowing the state to enforce the restrictions.[169] But in doing so, he also rejected the state's core argument that public school libraries are government speech.[170] This litigation continues, in Iowa and elsewhere, but publishers are eyeing other possibilities. "Where I'm looking to come in is on the legislative side," said Rosalie Stewart, a Penguin Random House public policy manager whose newly created job includes pushing back against book bans. "Where we really have an opportunity now is in freedom-to-read legislation, legislation that's going to protect our authors' right to be read. It's going to protect students who need access to diverse materials, and it's going to protect teachers and librarians." She hopes that state-level legislation might head off book banning challenges that have started cropping up in public and school libraries even in states with Democratic governments.[171]

At the same time, book banning activists are weaponizing the book "weeding" processes through which libraries maintain their collections. The Library Bill of Rights states that weeding should not be used as a deselection tool for controversial materials. Yet officials in New York's Nassau County have allegedly done precisely this, weeding *Ghost Boys*, about a Black boy shot by white police officers; *Almost Perfect*, a transgender love story; and *And Tango Makes Three*, the picture book about a penguin raised by two male penguins. Where challenging books usually requires a public process, weeding takes place behind closed doors, ensuring that books quietly disappear.

"When you remove a book because you believe it [advocates] critical race theory, or portrays LGBTQ lives or because you believe it's too vulgar, that's not weeding," said Deborah Caldwell-Stone, director of the American Library Association's Office for Intellectual Freedom. "That's censorship."[172]

In weaponizing the weeding process, conservative book banners appear to be embracing a strategy that progressives have employed for some time. The 2023 mass book purge in Ontario's Peel District schools was characterized as "weeding." Moreover, some librarians are reluctant to acquire books that they find deeply problematic. When reports indicated that Simon & Schuster would publish a book by right-wing provocateur Milo Yiannopoulos, librarians took to Library Think Tank, a Facebook group, to debate whether libraries should acquire it. "Some librarians stated that they would never buy the book while others said that they owed it to their community members to have the book in their collections," according to information sciences scholar Emily Knox.[173] Still, individual librarians are usually bound by board-level materials selection policies and often have only a limited say in what ends up on the shelves.

* * *

IF THERE IS anything salutary to be gleaned from the attacks on libraries, it is a renewed appreciation for why they matter.

Libraries have long provided vital intellectual infrastructure to liberal democracies. In the eighteenth century, Benjamin Franklin argued that libraries were an engine of social mobility and cultural self-fashioning. In the nineteenth century, Andrew Carnegie donated much of his fortune to constructing libraries around the world: "There is not such a cradle of democracy on earth as the free public library," he said. In the twentieth century, the American Library Association further solidified the link between the library and democracy by formalizing a commitment to intellectual freedom. Today, however, some argue that the library no longer serves democracy as it once did.

Our cultural attitudes about books and reading have changed over time, and libraries have changed with them. Libraries once framed their mission in terms of educating the "common man" and providing access to cultural products that were presumed to be spiritually ennobling. But we no longer see culture in such lofty terms. The old hierarchy separating "high" and "low" art came to be seen as arbitrary and elitist. We've long accepted that television shows, comic books, and video games are as worthy of study and aesthetic contemplation as opera, poetry, or literary fiction. Aligned with public demand, libraries shifted their focus from edification to entertainment. (The Toronto Public Library [TPL] currently has 65 physical copies of *Prophet Song*, Paul Lynch's 2023 Booker Prize–winning novel, and 220 physical copies of *Camino Ghost*, John Grisham's latest bestseller.) Rather than presuming to dictate what the reading public "needs," they responded to what the public wants. Who were librarians—or professors, critics, or anyone else, for that matter—to tell the public what it should read?[174]

Over this period, libraries were evolving to meet other pressing needs. Today, libraries help immigrants with ESL classes, résumés, job searches, and citizenship test preparation. They offer workshops on tenants' rights, computer literacy, personal finance, and small business accounting. They provide space for people who are poor, unhoused, or otherwise vulnerable, and internet access for anyone who needs it.

Some see these developments as evidence that twenty-first century democracies have outgrown libraries. Even if its public services are essential, they argue, there's no reason why libraries—as opposed to community centres, shelters, or purpose-built amenities—couldn't fulfill those services. Moreover, say the library's critics, it's not obvious what feeding the public (including middle- and upper-class people who can afford to buy books) an endless supply of James Patterson or Colleen Hoover novels contributes to the cause of democracy. Besides, most of the books and documents that could be seen as conducive to democracy are freely available online.* Why do we need libraries?

There's no denying that much of the library's business has shifted online. While the Toronto Public Library still loans slightly more physical than electronic materials—there were 12,679,379 physical checkouts in 2023, compared to 12,313,520 electronic ones—electronic circulation saw a 14% increase over the prior year, while physical loans saw an almost 20% decrease.[175] The rise of e-books raises troubling questions for libraries, especially because they do not *own* these books: Rather, they temporarily license user access from corporations like OverDrive. Acquiring e-book distribution rights can be more expensive than buying print versions, and those licenced books come with expiration dates. As the *New Yorker*'s Daniel A. Gross points out, the prospect of expiring libraries—where collections are akin to the "libraries" of content temporarily available on Netflix or YouTube—undercuts one of the library's crucial roles. "The point of

....

* Kenneth Whyte asserts as much in a provocative *Globe and Mail* opinion piece, "Throwing the book at libraries." His main point, worth taking seriously, is that libraries work against the economic interests of writers, publishers, and booksellers.

a library is to preserve," Gross argues, "and in order to preserve, a library must own."[176]

Of course, physical books don't last forever, either. But the materiality of books, especially those preserved in library reference and archival holdings, stand in opposition to the ephemerality of virtual culture. Recent history shows that online books can disappear for a variety of reasons. In 2020, the Internet Archive's nonprofit Open Library program, which allowed readers to borrow scanned copies of books, removed wait-lists to allow for increased access during the pandemic. In response, four major publishers sued the company for violating fair use law.[177] The Internet Archive lost on appeal and has since removed more than 500,000 of its online titles.[178] Meanwhile, libraries around the world have been subject to cyberattacks, which can disrupt their digital services and effectively bar patrons from accessing books. In 2023, criminals encrypted the Toronto Public Library's computer systems, stole employee data, and disabled its website; staff resorted to analog solutions, writing down bar codes with pen and paper, so that lending could continue.[179]

While we can debate whether today's libraries are over-indexing on entertainment or providing the right balance of public services, libraries remain essential. Democracies cannot entrust their intellectual infrastructure to the whims of tech billionaires and Silicon Valley venture capitalists. Prospective authoritarians would like nothing more than temporary, expiring libraries. While techno-utopians argue that we've outgrown "paywalled dead trees," that everything we need is online, the highly unfree state of the internet in China, Myanmar, Russia, and Iran—as measured through obstacles to access, limits on content (filtering and blocking websites and news sources), and violations of user rights (including surveillance, legal prosecution, and imprisonment)—should disabuse us of the fantasy of safe, permanent online alternatives to libraries. Imagine the ease of book banning if it were a mere matter of "unsubscribing" a title from an entire jurisdiction, or deleting entire virtual libraries with a few lines of code.

As historian Lucien Polastron reminds us, a great collection of books is, in its nature, inimical to totalitarian power. Libraries are the physical instantiation of expressive freedom, which Frederick Douglass called "the dread of tyrants ... the right which they first of all strike down."[180] At a moment in which, according to Freedom House's annual Freedom on the Net report, only 19 of the 72 countries they measured enjoy a "free" internet[181]—and at a moment in which global democratic freedom declined for the eighteenth consecutive year[182]—it seems particularly naïve to assume that our democratic and cultural inheritances are permanently safe online. Standing in opposition to the totalitarian dream of erasure (and the ephemeral nature of self-expiring virtual libraries) are physical books and the libraries that continue to collect and preserve them.

* * *

PUBLIC AND SCHOOL libraries are likely to remain the front lines for debates about the nature of our society and what we owe one another as citizens. If those debates become heated, that is not only because as taxpayers we all feel a sense of ownership over these institutions, but

also because we recognize libraries as symbolic representations of our community—spaces in which we are forced
to negotiate different and sometimes competing values.
Real-world conflicts can lead to intractable dilemmas.

In June 2023, Pride month, a teacher in the Ottawa-
Carleton District School Board distributed a widely used
LGBTQ+ support booklet, *I Am Muslim And I Might Not Be
Straight*, which was also posted on the school board's website, to students in her grade five-six class. The booklet
assured students that "you can still be Muslim if you are
Queer ... You are definitely not harraam (forbidden)," and
cited the prophet Muhammad as encouraging "open conversations about sex and desire" in the context of "unlearning
shame" and practising consensual sex.[183]

A parental backlash ensued, with Muslim community
members arguing that they had been unfairly singled
out.[184] The board faced a choice between the intellectual
freedom of (especially queer) students or responding to
accusations of discrimination from parents representing
a religious minority. In this case, the board censored
itself, removing the booklet from the LGBTQ+ resources
page of its website.[185]

This incident was just one manifestation of a larger
tension. Conservative Muslims have been pushing back
against LGBTQ+ content in schools across North America.
In May 2023, dozens of Islamic religious leaders signed a
public statement calling out the "increasing push to promote LGBTQ-centric values among children." This
statement, "Navigating Differences: Clarifying Sexual
and Gender Ethics in Islam"—which included signatories
from the Muslim Association of Canada, the Canadian
Council of Imams, and other groups—declared, in no

uncertain terms, that Islam condemns homosexuality. It
further stated that Islam forbids gender "affirming" or
"confirming" medical procedures, categorically rejected
"attempt[s] to reinterpret Islamic texts in favor of LGBTQ
affirmation," and opposes policies that "subvert the
agency of Muslim parents." In its opening section, the
statement characterizes Islam as "a religious minority
that frequently experiences bigotry and exclusion," which
is to say that the appeal is framed as the request of an
equity-seeking group.[186]

The religious authorities behind "Navigating Differences" don't speak for all Muslims, just as the Floridians
who invoke the gospels to ban LGBTQ+ literature don't
speak for all Christians. Increasingly, however, Muslim and
Christian conservatives have joined ranks in their opposition to the teaching of "gender ideology" in schools,
marching and demonstrating in cities across North America, hoisting placards reading "Let Kids Be Kids" and "No
Puberty Blocker for My Child." Calls for book banning are
ubiquitous in these circles: Activists use WhatsApp and
Facebook groups to circulate unverified viral videos alleg-
ing that schools are pushing sexually explicit books or
teaching children to masturbate.[187] In Minnesota, hundreds of Muslim families threatened to pull their children
from school in an "attendance strike" over LGBTQ+ books.[188]

Such conflicts force libraries to calibrate their long-
standing dedication to intellectual freedom with their
more recent commitment to promoting equity. These
priorities may not be entirely compatible; at the very
least, they speak in different registers. TPL's "Intellectual
Freedom Statement" is rooted in liberal universalism. It
speaks to the rights of individuals, not groups. It promises

"universal access" to "all points of view" and "all sides." It champions equality and sameness. TPL's "Equity Statement," meanwhile, is rooted in the ethos of progressivism. It speaks of an intersectional commitment to group categories: race, sex, gender identity, gender expression, sexual orientation, and religious affiliation.* It is premised on providing an inequality of service based on the needs of equity-deserving groups—who have, in various contexts, invoked their status as a veto over the intellectual freedom of others. LGBTQ+ groups have argued that including Abigail Shrier's *Irreversible Damage* on library shelves harms trans people, while conservative Muslims argue that the promotion of LGBTQ+ content is a form of religious discrimination that infringes upon their rights as parents. The TPL asserts that "equity and intellectual freedom are mutually reinforcing," but it's not clear why this is so; indeed, appeals to equity can be used to undermine the commitment to intellectual freedom.

When faced with these conflicts in the form of actual book challenges, libraries across North America have mostly stood firm. Their message is: We do not censor. They do their best to advance equity and intellectual freedom, despite the imperfect alignment of those categories. They face innumerable internal and external challenges. "You've got staff that are challenging you. You've got politicians that are challenging you," said Linda Hazzan, TPL's Director for Communications, Programming and Customer Engagement. "It becomes a very emotional conversation instead of a philosophical or a policy conversation."[189]

....

* Which is complicated by the fact that no single representative speaks on behalf of these groups.

Obviously, book banning is an extraordinary waste of resources. Less obvious is the toll it exacts on librarians. When they stand their ground against book banners, librarians have been threatened with lawsuits and harassed with bogus accusations of pedophilia. Some fear going to work, never knowing when the book banning brigade will arrive. The banners disseminate book lists, email addresses, and phone numbers, and instruct followers to "bombard" libraries and municipal councils. Christine Ronceray, a Manitoba mother who argues that *All Boys Aren't Blue* constitutes pornography, emphasizes the importance of contacting libraries and politicians "every day." "Bombard—they need to hear this. We need to apply the pressure," she said on a podcast. The hope is that, eventually, librarians will give in.[190]

Thus far, most public libraries have not given in. "You shouldn't have to access a random website to read about having your period or about dating the people you want to date," says Lisa Radha Vohra of the TPL. Vohra's institution is solidly behind intellectual freedom, but she is intensely aware of the stakes involved—particularly for colleagues in countries where authoritarianism is ascendant. Those colleagues "are afraid to do their jobs," Vohra told me. Librarians have been fired, and in some cases killed, over the books on their shelves.

"No one should be threatened for providing access to information," Vohra says, her voice cracking with emotion. "I'm not so naïve to think it couldn't happen here."[191]

* * *

THIS BOOK HAS argued that adherents of the new censor-ship consensus, the progressive and religious fundamentalists who reduce literature to its ideological content, must be confronted with the facts of their behaviour. They are book banners. They have earned their place in the annals of censorship. They had their reasons; doubtless many still believe they are morally unimpeachable. But their censorship hastens the erosion of the civil values that undergird our society, which is why we can't allow it to continue. It is not for them to refash-ion public spaces according to their private beliefs. It is not for them, as Lindsay Durtschi, the Pensacola mother, put it, to "tell me what my kid can and can't read."

Expressive freedom is the condition that makes both art and democracy possible. It is also extraordinarily frag-ile—an objective fiction that exists only insofar as we believe in it and deem it worth fighting for. But with the righteous adherents of the censorship consensus dou-bling down on book banning as a tactic, and arguments for expressive freedom increasingly coded as reactionary or naïve, it seems entirely plausible that we will live to witness the slow fade-out of expressive freedom. This would be in keeping with history, where this freedom has only ever been the exception.

If this trend is reversible, it will require tireless effort on multiple fronts. State-sponsored censorship must be vigorously opposed in the courts. Lawmakers and lobbyists need to keep pushing "freedom to read" legisla-tion wherever it can be passed. Our institutions must rededicate themselves to intellectual freedom. The work of correcting historical wrongs and ameliorating social inequality needn't involve censorship and book banning,

although it will involve thoughtful approaches to teaching challenging books. Our educators are up to this task
but must be allowed to try.

Teachers, no less than librarians, need our support,
the broadest form of which involves a recommitment to
robust public funding for schools and their libraries. We
can also help teachers by sharpening the line between the
public sphere of the school and the private sphere of the
home. Parents are justified in calls for curricular transparency, but not in imposing their own beliefs upon that
curriculum or on the school library. In jurisdictions
including Ontario, parents are entitled to far greater
transparency around library holdings than is currently
available. If our school boards are unwilling to stop weeding library books based on content, parents and politicians
will have to push for increased accountability in the form
of searchable library catalogues. Just as parents must
respect transparent processes when it comes to challenging books, so, too, should our institutions.

In renegotiating the norms around public and private
spheres, we also need to think carefully about the scope of
education within highly diverse, pluralistic democracies.
We need to be clear on what it is that teachers teach. And
what they teach are subjects, with age-appropriate learning
objectives aimed at developing student competencies.
When parents accuse educators of "indoctrination," as they
will, educators need to be able to look them in the eye and
explain that education is not indoctrination: The first
involves the building of critical thinking abilities, the second involves breaking them down. The first involves
developing skills and capacity for independent thought
within a field of study; the second involves blind submission

to a doctrine that must be accepted without criticism or question. Teachers must be empowered to teach about historical and present forms of injustice, and to empower their own students to identify and think critically about the sources of indoctrination everywhere vying for their attention. Public education and indoctrination are mutually exclusive: The integrity of the former hinges upon its repudiation of the latter.

School libraries are different from public libraries in important ways, and their selection policies must reflect the diverse needs of contemporary students. While they must uphold strict limits against pseudo-scientific, conspiratorial or historically inaccurate material that is permissible in public libraries, school libraries must also take seriously their commitments to upholding intellectual freedom. That freedom entails the right to "seek and receive information from all points of view without restriction," according to the American Library Association. To make good on that promise, library collections must actually represent those different points of view. Libraries cannot uphold intellectual freedom while aggressively weeding "problematic" resources and limiting all new acquisitions to material that supports a single, totalizing ideological program. School libraries must, therefore, provide a reasonable range of age-appropriate perspectives, while also respecting that students read in different ways, for different reasons. We cannot allow the school library to become a mechanism for enforcing ideological conformity.

We must also do a better job of educating students on the importance of expressive freedom—an understanding of which is vital to negotiating the chaotic information landscapes they will inhabit. And in educating students on the value of their own intellectual freedom, the liberal tradition remains indispensable. We defend free speech not to hear the sounds of our own voices, but for the necessity of hearing the voices of others. People have always argued that one book or another must be banned to stop the circulation of harmful ideas; it was ever thus. Centuries ago, John Milton showed that suppressing erroneous and morally dubious books does little to stem the spread of bad ideas. Further, he revealed why virtuous ideas must be tested against their opposites, and that our moral truths emerge from internal deliberations, not from the dictates of external authorities. In the writings of Frederick Douglass, we find a powerful articulation of the idea that totalitarianism cannot coexist with intellectual freedom, which is why dictators and aspiring authoritarians will always have one eye on your books.

J. S. Mill reminds us that our only mechanism for achieving certainty is trial and disputation, which means that we depend upon the free speech of those with whom we disagree. Even if a vast majority of people concur with our desire to censor an outlier, censorship is still wrong, because the power itself is illegitimate. Censorship doesn't have to eradicate every copy of a book to work: preventing a single child from accessing a single book is wrong enough. Censorship can be spectacular in its devastation, destroying lives and impoverishing humanity by robbing us of precious monuments of creative expression. But its harms are not always visible or even tangible, and may include depriving children of the opportunity to better know themselves through literature.

The public value of literature—especially imaginative literature—has rarely felt more precarious than it does today, and book banning thrives when we are unable to articulate the value of reading it. Two years ago, during my crisis of confidence in an elementary school library, I struggled to explain that value, even to myself. Literature, I felt and still feel, is our most powerful technology for self-transcendence, for representing psychological interiority, for knowing more people, and in more ways, than our embodied lives could ever allow. But literature's pleasures cannot be reduced to encountering otherness, for they also include that simple, uncanny sensation that Vladimir Nabokov called "aesthetic bliss": the goosebumps, the tingle at the base of the skull, produced by those magical appositions of sound and sense. Yet literature isn't reducible to this pleasure either. For there are the vast gratifications of tradition, of grappling with the wisdom of the ages, of assembling the fragments. Quite separately, there are the soulful pleasures of deep reading—of developing focus and attention through sustained engagement. But it's not reducible to that, either.

And that's just it: Literature isn't reducible—not to summaries or quotations, or to any of these pleasures or values or states of being. And reducing literature is precisely what censorship does: With its ideological checklists or puritanical frameworks, it reduces literature to a shrunken, misshapen parody of itself. A novel teeming with voices and perspectives becomes a single "message," or a wicked idea, a naughty image, or even a single, abominable word. Alternatively, it is judged according to the supposed virtues it didn't fulfill, the boxes it failed to tick, as though such boxes reveal anything—as though they exist.

We live, as the euphemism has it, in polarized times. Do we believe that any censor will be less biased than the

Fox or CNN or CBC anchors who deliver our news, the journalists, the academics, the Supreme Court justices? Could any censor hope to step outside of that cultural inferno? Of course not. Any hypothetical censor will be every bit as biased as the rest of us, and we'll know it, and our polarization, our anger, will harden along with our ignorance. If censorship will aid anyone, it will aid those who are already in positions of power.

Liberalism can't hide from its failures. Critics aren't wrong to point out the shortcomings and hypocrisies of the foundational thinkers of expressive freedom. Milton was prejudiced against Catholics; J. S. Mill supported and worked on behalf of English colonialism in India. These failings no more invalidate the ideal of expressive freedom than Albert Einstein's cruelty toward his wife invalidates the theory of relativity. But those failings may, if we let them, complete the process of our demoralization. This is one path. We accept that the past is irretrievably corrupt, poisoned from the root. The guttering candle sizzles out for another age.

Or we take another look at the old books. They are tattered and dog-eared, full of unfamiliar words and ungainly sentences too long for our withered attention spans. We find that they were written by human hands, fashioned by people riven with imperfections and biases, flaws that just might help us identify our own. Their failings become part of the story, but not the end of the story, which we inherit, revise, and humbly resubmit to the readers who succeed us.

Acknowledgments

MY FIRST THANKS go to Will Di Novi, who invited me to deliver a lecture series on book banning, and to Ian Williams, who encouraged me to imagine those lectures as a book. I'm deeply grateful to Sarmishta Subramanian for commissioning and editing an early part of this work for the *Toronto Star* (and for much else). Joel Goldbach read a complete draft of the manuscript and offered transformative feedback. Thanks also to Paul Downes, Tony Ricci, Kelly Baron, Tim Perry, and Lisa Radha Vohra. My sincere thanks to the Biblioasis team: Vanessa Stauffer, Chandra Wohleber, Ingrid Paulson, and especially Dan Wells for believing in this book and for greatly enriching it with his editorial feedback. This book is dedicated to my children, Grace and Sam, who know the power of reading and already exhibit a healthy distrust of authority.

Notes

1   Alexandra Alter, "Book Bans Continue to Surge in Public Schools," *The New York Times*, April 16, 2024 https://www.nytimes.com/2024/04/16/books/book-bans-public-schools.html

2   Kasey Meehan and Jonathan Friedman, "Banned in the USA: State Laws Supercharge Book Suppression in Schools," PEN *America*, April 20, 2023.

3   Brenda Cossman, "Censor, Resist, Repeat: A History of Censorship of Gay and Lesbian Sexual Representation in Canada," *Duke Journal of Gender, Law & Policy* 21.1 (2013).

4   See *Rosen v. United States* (1896), qtd. in Jennifer Elaine Steele, "A History of Censorship in the United States," *Journal of Intellectual Freedom and Privacy* 5.1 (2020): https://journals.ala.org/index.php/jifp/article/view/7208/10293.

5   "Moms for Liberty," Southern Poverty Law Center, https://www.splcenter.org/fighting-hate/extremist-files/group/moms-liberty.

6   Joseph Brean, "Toronto school board's N-word ban targets white authors like Steinbeck, Twain," *National Post*, January 10, 2024, https://nationalpost.com/feature/toronto-school-board-bans-n-word.

7   Nicole Brockbank, Angelina King, "'Empty shelves with absolutely no books': Students, parents question school board's library weeding process," CBC News, https://www.cbc.ca/news/canada/toronto/peel-school-board-library-book-weeding-1.6964332.

8   Elizabeth Blair, "What's a book ban anyway? Depends on who you ask," NPR, June 10, 2024, https://www.npr.org/2024/06/04/nx-s1-4941240/book-bans-schools-libraries-censorship#:~:text=Kasey%20Meehan%2C%20program%20director%20of,access%20to%20a%20book%20ois.

9   "Collection Maintenance and Weeding," American Library Association, https://www.ala.org/tools/challengesupport/selectionpolicytoolkit/weeding.

10 Jay P. Greene, Max Eden, and Madison Marino, "The Book Ban Mirage," American Enterprise Institute, https://www.aei.org/wp-content/uploads/2023/07/EFI-Book_Ban_Mirage-2.pdf?x85095&x91208.

11 Dave Seminara, "The Left Twists the Meaning of 'Book Ban," *City Journal*, June 26, 2023, https://www.city-journal.org/article/the-left-twists-the-meaning-of-book-ban.

12 Bob Armstrong, "A Likely Story: The 'Diversity' Myth Consumes the Canadian Literary Scene," *C2C Journal*, March 2, 2024.

13 Jennifer Smith, "Random House Canada staff try to ban Jordan Peterson's New Book," *Daily Mail*, November 25, 2022, https://www.dailymail.co.uk/news/article-8985983/Random-House-Canada-try-ban-Jordan-Petersons-new-book.html.

14 As of this writing in November 2024, the Tundra submissions policy advises writers from non-underrepresented communities to keep an eye on social media to know "if and when" submissions will open up more broadly. https://tundrabooks.com/submissions/.

15 Elizabeth Blair, "What's a book ban anyway? Depends on who you ask," NPR, June 10, 2024, https://www.npr.org/2024/06/04/nx-s1-4941240/book-bans-schools-libraries-censorship#:~:text=Kasey%20Meehan%2C%20program%20director%20of,access%20to%20a%20book%20is.

16 "Materials Selection Policy," Toronto Public Library, effective January 23, 2023, https://www.torontopubliclibrary.ca/terms-of-use/library-policies/materials-selection-policy.jsp.

17 Ibid.

18 "A Guide to the Selection and Deselection of School Library Resources," Ontario School Library Association, July 31, 2023, https://accessola.com/wp-content/uploads/2023/09/FINAL-2023-09-OSLA-A-Guide-to-the-Selection-and-Deselection-of-School-Library-Resources_EN.pdf.

19 Anita Brooks Kirkland, "Balance or Indoctrination: Developing and Defending Balanced School Library Collections," *Canadian School Libraries Journal* (May 22, 2024): https://journal.canadianschoollibraries.ca/balance-or-indoctrination-developing-and-defending-balanced-school-library-collections/.

20 Elizabeth A. Harris and Alexandra Alter, "A Fast-Growing Network of Conservative Groups is Fueling a Surge in Book Bans," *The New York Times*, December 12, 2022, https://www.nytimes.com/2022/12/12/books/book-bans-libraries.html.

21 Amy Judd and Travis Prasad, "Books pulled from B.C. district curriculum in what premier calls 'crazy decision,'" Global News, March 1, 2024, https://globalnews.ca/news/10326701/bc-school-district-pulls-books-curriculum-content/.

22 Andrew Van Dam, "How many books did you read in 2023?" *The Washington Post*, January 5, 2024.

23 Rose Horowitch, "The Elite College Students Who Can't Read Books," *The Atlantic*, October 1, 2024, https://www.theatlantic.com/magazine/archive/2024/11/the-elite-college-students-who-cant-read-books/679945/.

24 Lincoln Michel, "Yes, People Still Buy Books," *Slate*, April 30, 2024, https://slate.com/culture/2024/04/book-sales-publishing-industry-statistics-substack-penguin-lawsuit.html

25 "Media Education in English Langauge Arts," National Council of Teachers of English, April 9, 2022, https://ncte.org/statement/media_education/.

26 "American Time Use Summary," U.S. Bureau of Labor Statistics, June 27, 2024, https://www.bls.gov/news.release/atus.nr0.htm.

27 "Constant Companion: A Week in the Life of a Young Person's Smartphone Use," Common Sense Media, 2023, https://www.commonsensemedia.org/sites/default/files/research/report/2023-cs-smartphone-research-report_final-for-web.pdf.

28 Quoted in Frederick H. Cramer, "Bookburning and Censorship in Ancient Rome: A Chapter from the History of Freedom of Speech," *Journal of the History of Ideas* 6.2 (1945): 157–96.

29 Lee Ying Shan, "Salman Rushdie's 'The Satanic Verses' leaps to the top of Amazon's bestseller lists," CNBC, August 15, 2022, https://www.cnbc.com/2022/08/16/salman-rushdies-books-top-amazons-bestseller-lists-after-stabbing.html.

30 Robin Vose, *The Index of Prohibited Books* (London: Reaktion, 2022), p. 147.

31 Mark Edmundson, "Good People: The New Discipline," *Liberties* 3.4 (Summer 2023): https://libertiesjournal.com/articles/good-people-the-new-discipline/.

32 Ali Swenson, Will Weissert, and Moriah Balingit, "Trump holds 'fireside chat' at Moms for Liberty summit in Washington, D. C.," PBS News, August 31, 2024, https://www.pbs.org/newshour/politics/watch-live-trump-addresses-moms-for-liberty-summit-in-washington-dc.

33 Ligaya Mishan, "The Long and Tortured History of Cancel Culture," *The New York Times Style Magazine*, December 3, 2020, https://www.nytimes.com/2020/12/03/t-magazine/cancel-culture-history.html.

34 Isaac Chotiner, "Why Did the New York Review of Books Publish that Jian Ghomeshi Essay?" *Slate*, September 14, 2018, https://slate.com/news-and-politics/2018/09/jian-ghomeshi-new-york-review-of-books-essay.html.

35 John Williams, "New York Review of Books Acknowledges 'Failures' in a #MeToo Essay," *The New York Times*, September 24, 2018, https://www.nytimes.com/2018/09/24/books/jian-bui-uma-review-of-books.html.

36 Kenneth Whyte, "Not all Conservatives are philistines. They should help fix Canada's broken cultural system," *The Globe and Mail*, Febuary 6, 2021, https://www.theglobeandmail.com/opinion/article-not-all-conservatives-are-philistines-they-should-help-fix-canadas/.

37 Anna Kornbluh explicates these trends in *Immediacy, or The Style of Too Late Capitalism* (London: Verso, 2024).

38 Andrew Marantz, "How Social-Media Trolls Turned U.C. Berkeley Into a Free-Speech Circus," *The New Yorker*, June 25, 2018, https://www.newyorker.com/magazine/2018/07/02/how-social-media-trolls-turned-uc-berkeley-into-a-free-speech-circus.

39 William Davies, "The free speech panic: how the right concocted a crisis," *The Guardian*, July 26, 2018, https://www.theguardian.com/news/2018/jul/26/the-free-speech-panic-censorship-how-the-right-concocted-a-crisis.

40 "A Letter on Justice and Open Debate," *Harper's*, July 7, 2020.

41 "A More Specific Letter on Justice and Open Debate," *The Objective*, July 10, 2020.

42 I intend here to echo the title and argument put forth by Astra Taylor in *Democracy May Not Exist, But We'll Miss It When It's Gone* (New York: Metropolitan Books, 2019).

43 C. S. Lewis, epilogue to *An Experiment in Criticism* (Cambridge: UP, 1961); Ursula K. Le Guin, "A Message About Messages," *CBC Magazine*, 2005, https://www.ursulakleguin.com/message-about-messages; Allan Bloom, *Giants and Dwarves* (New York: Simon and Schuster, 1990), 20.

44 Le Guin makes this point in the essay cited above.

45 Brooke Howard, "Florida School District Bans a Book on…Penguins," *The Daily Beast*, February 22, 2023.

46 Brittany Misencik, "School Board Bans Three Books: They Join Growing List in Escambia County Schools," *Pensacola News Journal*, February 22, 2023.

47 Brittany Misencik, "Escambia School Board votes to keep 4 challenged books after 7+ hours of debate," *Pensacola News Journal*, March 21, 2023, https://www.pnj.com/story/news/education/2023/03/21/escambia-school-board-keeps-4-challenged-books-after-7-hours-of-debate/70033181007/.

48 Ibid.

49 Brittany Misencik, "'This is child pornography': SR school board candidate takes book concerns to Sheriff's Office," November 8, 2023, https://www.pnj.com/story/news/education/2023/11/08/school-board-candidate-calls-cops-on-librarians-over-pornographic-books/71487021007/.

50 Lisa Tolin, "More Than 1,600 Books Banned in Escambia County, Florida," PEN America, January 9, 2024. https://pen.org/escambia-county-florida-banned-books-list/#:~:text=Five%20dictionaries%20are%20on%20the,banning%20materials%20with%20"sexual%20conduct.

51 Kiara Alfonseca, "Book Ban Lawsuit Moves Forward as Florida District Removes over 1,000 Titles," ABC News, January 11, 2024, https://abcnews.go.com/US/book-ban-lawsuit-moves-forward-florida-district-removes/story?id=106292183.

52 Brittany Misencik, "'I Couldn't Be Quiet Anymore': Meet the Escambia County Mom Who Signed onto the Book Ban Lawsuit," *Pensacola News Journal*, May 31, 2023.

53 Isaac Arnsdorf, Doug Bock Clarke, Alexandra Berzon, and Anjeanette Damon, "Heeding Steve Bannon's Call, Election Deniers Organizer to Seize Control of the GOP—and Reshape America's Elections," ProPublica, September 2, 2021.

54 Jennifer C. Berkshire and Jack Schneider, "The GOP's School Board Takeover Strategy is Falling Flat," *The Hill*, July 25, 2022.

55 Alexander Panetta, "The backstory on a U.S. book-ban blitz and an unlikely target: A book about cute babies," CBC News, May 1, 2022, https://www.cbc.ca/news/world/everywhere-babies-backstory-1.6436594.

56 "Legislative Agenda," Florida Citizens Alliance, https://goflca.org/agenda/, accessed October 24, 2024.

57 Nikki Ross and Alia Wong, "Florida Ranks 2nd School Books Ban," *The New Press*, September 25, 2022.

58 No Left Turn in Education, https://www.noleftturn.us.

59 Example letters, No Left Turn in Education, https://www.noleftturn.us/example-letters/.

60 "Ban After Reading," *Harpers*, February 2024, https://harpers.org/archive/2024/02/ban-after-reading/.

61 CS/HB 1467 – K–12 Education, the Florida Senate, effective July 1, 2022, https://www.flsenate.gov/Committees/billsummaries/2022/html/2823.

62 "Governor Ron DeSantis Signs Bill that Requires Curriculum Transparency," Florida governor Ron DeSantis, March 25, 2022, https://www.flgov.com/2022/03/25/governor-ron-desantis-signs-bill-that-requires-curriculum-transparency/.

63 Jesse Kline, "Have some Jewish groups gone too far by trying to silence their opponents?" *The Canadian Jewish News*, October 18, 2017.

64 Ron DeSantis, "Exposing the Book Ban Hoax," https://www.flgov.com/2023/03/08/governor-ron-desantis-debunks-book-ban-hoax/.

65 https://www.flgov.com/2023/03/08/governor-ron-desantis-debunks-book-ban-hoax/.

66 Leslie Lopez, "Queer Books Save Lives: Fighting Book Censorship in Texas," *Oh Reader*, 2021, https://www.ohreader.com/queer-books-save-lives.

67 Nicole Brockbank and Angelina King, "'Empty shelves with absolutely no books': Students, parents question school board's library weeding process," CBC News, September 13, 2023, https://www.cbc.ca/news/canada/toronto/peel-school-board-library-book-weeding-1.6964332.

68 Ibid.

69 https://librariesnotlandfills.ca/wp-content/uploads/2023/08/Peel-Board-Book-Purge-Manual.pdf.

70 Margorie Gann, "Empty Shelves," *C2C Journal*, December 17, 2023, https://c2cjournal.ca/2023/12/empty-shelves-the-noxious-politics-behind-a-canadian-school-boards-massive-book-purge/.

71 https://cfe.torontomu.ca/bpc-bulletins/bpc-bulletin-book-purge-peel-regions-public-schools-2023.

72 Nicole Brockbank and Angelina King, "How teacher librarians interpreted GTA school board's controversial book-weeding process," October 31, 2023, https://www.cbc.ca/news/canada/toronto/teacher-librarians-speak-out-peel-school-book-weeding-1.7003363.

73 Ibid.

74 https://librariesnotlandfills.ca/wp-content/uploads/2023/08/Peel-Board-Book-Purge-Manual.pdf.

75 "A Guide to the Selection and Deselection of School Library Resources," Ontario School Library Association, 2023, https://accessola.com/wp-content/uploads/2023/09/FINAL-2023-09-OSLA-A-Guide-to-the-Selection-and-Deselection-of-School-Library-Resources_EN.pdf.

76 Nikki Ross and Alia Wong, "Florida Ranks 2nd School Books Ban," *The New Press*, September 25, 2022.

77 Frederick H. Cramer, "Bookburning and Censorship in Ancient Rome: A Chapter from the History of Freedom of Speech," *Journal of the History of Ideas* 6.2 (1945): 157–96.

78 Ibid.

79 Ibid.

80 Ibid.

81 Harriet I. Flowers, *The Art of Forgetting* (Chapel Hill: University of North Carolina Press, 2006).

82 Ibid.

83 Thomas K. Dix, "Private and Public Libraries at Rome in the First Century B.C.: A Preliminary Study in the History of Roman Libraries," PhD dissertation, University of Michigan, 1986.

84 Roy Macleod, "Introduction: Alexandria in History and Myth," in *The Library of Alexandria: Centre of Learning in the Ancient World*, ed. Roy Macleod (London: I. B. Tauris & Co, 2004), pp. 1–18.

85 Edward Gibbon, *History of the Decline and Fall of the Roman Empire*, vol. 3, chapter 28: Destruction of Paganism—Part II.

86 Macleod, op cit.

87 Pearce Carefoot, *Nihil obstat: An exhibition of banned, censored and challenged books in the West, 1491–2000*, Thomas Fisher Rare Book Library, Toronto, 2005).

88 Robin Vose, *The Index of Prohibited Books* (London: Reaktion, 2022), p. 155.

89 Amy Werbel, *Lust on Trial: Censorship and the Rise of American Obscenity in the Age of Anthony Comstock* (New York: Columbia University Press, 2018), p. 41.

90 Greg Lukianoff, Adam Goldstein, and Ryne Weiss, "'The Mind of the Censor and the Eye of the Beholder' introduces a new generation to the Infamous (and often absurd) Anthony Comstock," *FIRE*, November 1, 2021, https://www.thefire.org/news/blogs/eternally-radical-idea/mind-censor-and-eye-beholder-introduces-new-generation-infamous.

91 Ibid., p. 51.

92   Ibid., p. 19.

93   Werbel, *Lust on Trial*, p. 141.

94   Quoted in "'The Mind of the Censor and the Eye of the Beholder,'" pp. 63–64.

95   Richard Lingeman, *Theodore Dreiser: An American Journey* (New York: G. P. Putnam's Sons, 1990), p. 128.

96   "'The Mind of the Censor and the Eye of the Beholder,'" pp. 19–20.

97   Peter Galison, "Blacked-out spaces: Freud, censorship and the re-territorialization of mind," *The British Society for the History of Science* 45.2 (June 2012).

98   Lucien Polastron, *Books on Fire: The Destruction of Libraries Throughout History* (Rochester, Vermont: Inner Traditions, 2007), p. x.

99   Quoted in Rebecca Knuth, *Burning Books and Levelling Libraries* (Westport, Conn.: Praeger, 2006), p. 205.

100 Knuth, p. 206.

101 Rumsfeld quoted in Maureen Dowd, "A Tale of Two Fridays," *The New York Times*, April 20, 2003.

102 "'At the Instance of Benjamin Franklin': A Brief History of the Library Company of Philadelphia," The Library Company of Philadelphia, 2015, https://www.librarycompany.org/about/AttheInstance2015_98709140764695.pdf?_gl=1*16etxoz*_gcl_au*NTkwMDUxMzQuMTcyNzgwNTYwOQ..*_ga*NTg4ODkyNTY4LjE3Mjc4MDU2MDk.*_ga_TZ5N7E4ZT1*MTcyNzgwNTYwOS4xLjAuMTcyNzgwNTYwOS42MC4wLjA.

103 Elizabeth Webster, "How Ben Franklin Invented the Library as We Know It," *Smithsonian Magazine*, April/May 2024, https://www.smithsonianmag.com/history/how-ben-franklin-invented-library-as-we-know-it-180983983/.

104 Benjamin Franklin, *Autobiography*, ed. Frank Woodworth Pine, 1922, Project Gutenberg, https://www.gutenberg.org/files/20203/20203-h/20203-h.htm.

105 Peter Mickelson, "American Society and the Public Library in the Thought of Andrew Carnegie," *The Journal of Library History* 10.2 (1975): 117–38.

106 "Carnegie libraries in Ontario," Government of Ontario, https://www.ontario.ca/page/carnegie-libraries-ontario.

107 Kenneth Whyte, "Throwing the book at libraries," *The Globe and Mail*, July 25, 2020.

108 "Over 150 libraries surpass 1 million digital checkouts in 2023," OverDrive, January 11, 2024, https://company.overdrive.com/2024/01/11/2023-million-digital-checkouts/#:~:text=In%20total%2C%20662%20million%20ebooks,2023%20can%20be%20found%20here.

109 "The State of America's Libraries," American Library Association 2023 report, https://www.ala.org/sites/default/files/news/content/state-of-americas-libraries-report-2023-web-version.pdf.

110 David Hawkes, *John Milton: A Hero of Our Time* (Berkeley: Counterpoint, 2009), pp. 133, 134.

111 Quoted in Hawkes, *John Milton: A Hero of Our Time*.

112 Eunmi Park, "*Areopagitica* in the Licensing Controversy: Milton's Rhetorical Strategies and Modes," *Journal of British and American Studies* 10 (2004).

113 John Milton, *Areopagitica: A Speech of Mr. John Milton for the Liberty of Unlicenc'd Printing to the Parlament of England*, ed. Thomas H. Huxon, *The John Milton Reading Room* (Dartmouth College), https://milton.host.dartmouth.edu/reading_room/areopagitica/text.shtml.

114 Quoted in David French, "When TikTok's Algorithm Turns Deadly," *The New York Times*, September 8, 2024.

115 Kai Ruggeri et al. "Behavioural interventions to reduce vaccine hesitancy driven by misinformation on social media," BMJ 2024; 384.

116 "Did Biden's White House pressure Mark Zukerberg to censor COVID content?" *Al Jazeera*, August 27, 2024, https://www.aljazeera.com/news/2024/8/27/did-bidens-white-house-pressure-mark-zuckerberg-to-censor-covid-content.

117 "Covid origin: Why the Wuhan lab-leak theory is so disputed," BBC News, March 1, 2023, https://www.bbc.com/news/world-asia-china-57268111.

118 Hunt Allcott and Matthew Gentzkow, "Social Media and Fake News in the 2016 Election," *Journal of Economic Perspectives*, 31.2, Spring 2017.

119 Jacob Mchangama, *Free Speech: A History from Socrates to Social Media* (New York: Basic Books, 2022), 387-88.

120 Richard Reeves, *John Stuart Mill: Victorian Firebrand* (London: Atlantic Books, 2007), p. 260.

121 Ibid., pp. 260–61.

122 John Stuart Mill, *On Liberty* (London: Longmans, Green, Reader and Dyer, 1859) Project Gutenberg, http://www.gutenberg.org/files/34901/34901-h/34901-h.htm.

123 Frederick Douglass, "A Plea for Free Speech in Boston" (1860), National Constitution Center, https://constitutioncenter.org/the-constitution/historic-document-library/detail/frederick-douglass-a-plea-for-free-speech-in-boston-1860.

124 "Hit Man Manual," Free Speech Center at Middle Tennessee State University, https://firstamendment.mtsu.edu/article/hit-man-manual/.

125 U.S. National Archives, Alien and Sedition Acts (1798), https://www.archives.gov/milestone-documents/alien-and-sedition-acts#:~:text=The%20Sedition%20Act%20made%20it,typically%20favored%20by%20new%20citizens.

126 "Sedition Law Passes," Library of Congress, https://www.loc.gov/exhibitions/world-war-i-american-experiences/about-this-exhibition/over-here/surveillance-and-censorship/sedition-law-passes/.

127 Edward De Grazia, *Censorship Landmarks* (New York: R. R. Bowker Company, 1969).

128 Quoted in Brett Gary, *Dirty Works: Obscenity on Trial in America's First Sexual Revolution* (Stanford: Stanford University Press, 2021), p. 182. My rendering of the *Ulysses* case is indebted to Gary's reconstruction of the trial.

129 Gary, *Dirty Works*, p. 210.

130 De Grazia, *Censorship Landmarks*.

131 *Miller v. California*, Oyez, www.oyez.org/cases/1971/70-73.

132 G. C. Lisby, "'Trying to Define What May Be Indefinable': The Georgia Literature Commission, 1953–1973," *The Georgia Historical Quarterly* 84.1 (2000).

133 Brenda Cossman, "Censor, Resist, Repeat: A History of Censorship of Gay and Lesbian Sexual Representation in Canada," *Duke Journal of Gender, Law & Policy* 21.1, (2013).

134 Cossman tells the story of *The Body Politic*'s prosecution in "Censor, Resist, Repeat"; I've also consulted contemporary newspaper accounts in the *Toronto Star* and elsewhere.

135 Cossman, p. 49.

136 Quoted in Cossman, "Censor, Resist, Repeat," p. 55.

137 Ibid.

138 https://x.com/chasestrangio/status/1327287611610763264?lang=en.

139 "Sale or Distribution of Harmful Materials to Minors," Georgia Senate Bill 154, https://www.legis.ga.gov/legislation/64318.

140 PDSB book weeding training document, https://librariesnotlandfills.ca/wp-content/uploads/2023/08/Peel-Board-Book-Purge-Manual.pdf.

141 Ibid.

142 Mari J. Matsuda, Charles R. Lawrence III, Richard Delgado, and Kimberlé Williams Crenshaw, introduction to *Words That Wound: Critical Race Theory, Assaultive Speech, and the First Amendment* (Boulder: Westview Press, 1993).

143 *Words That Wound*, p. 95

144 Ibid., pp. 24, 92.

145 Robert Beauregard, "PW talks with Arline Geronimus: Worn Out," *Publishers Weekly*, January 30, 2023.

146 PDSB book weeding training document, https://librariesnotlandfills.ca/wp-content/uploads/2023/08/Peel-Board-Book-Purge-Manual.pdf.

147 "A Guide to the Selection and Deselection of School Library Resources," Ontario School Library Association, 2023, https://accessola.com/wp-content/uploads/2023/09/FINAL-2023-09-OSLA-A-Guide-to-the-Selection-and-Deselection-of-School-Library-Resources_EN.pdf.

148 Henry Louis Gates Jr., Anthony P. Griffin, Donald E. Lively, Robert C. Post, William B. Rubenstein, and Nadine Strossen, *Speaking of Race, Speaking of Sex: Hate Speech, Civil Rights, and Civil Liberties* (New York: NYU Press, 1994), p. 41.

149 Ibid., p. 234.

150 Ibid., p. 45.

151 Timothy Garton Ash, *Free Speech: Ten Principles for a Connected World* (New Haven: Yale UP, 2016), p. 220.

152 Darragh Roche, "Pat Robertson Faces Backlash After Calling Critical Race Theory 'Monstrous Evil,'" *Newsweek*, June 26, 2021, https://www.newsweek.com/pat-robertson-faces-backlash-calling-critical-race-theory-monstrous-evil-1604379.

153 "Critical Race Theory Has Infiltrated the Federal Government, Christopher Rufo on Fox News," https://www.youtube.com/watch?v=rBXRdWflV7M.

154 Jake Lahut, "Fox News has mentioned 'critical race theory' nearly 1300 times since March, according to watchdog study," *Business Insider*, https://www.businessinsider.com/fox-news-critical-race-theory-mentions-thousand-study-2021-6.

155 Ta-Nehisi Coates, *The Message* (New York: One World, 2024), pp. 12–13.

156 Roosevelt Montás, *Rescuing Socrates: How the Great Books Changed My Life and Why They Matter for a New Generation* (Princeton: Princeton University Press, 2021).

157 Allan Bloom, *Giants and Dwarves* (New York: Simon and Schuster, 1990), p. 27.

158 Robert Post, "Racist Speech, Democracy, and the First Amendment," in *Speaking of Race, Speaking of Sex*, p. 116.

159 Adrian Johnston, Boštjan Nedoh, and Alenka Zupančič, eds., *Objective Fictions: Philosophy, Psychoanalysis, Marxism* (Edinburgh: Edinburgh University Press, 2022).

160 "Record Number of Writers Jailed Worldwide in 2023," PEN America, May 1, 2024, https://pen.org/press-release/record-number-of-writers-jailed-worldwide -in-2023/.

161 I am grateful to University of Toronto Professor Paul Downes for this point.

162 Erin Alberty, "Book banning activists target Little Free Libraries in Utah," *Axios*, October 4, 2024, https://www.axios.com/local/salt-lake-city/2024/ 10/04/book-ban-little-free-libraries-utah.

163 Laura Miller, "We Are a Relatively Easy Punching Bag," *Slate*, October 3, 2024.

164 Olivia Empson, "Activists 'fight against censorship' in the largest US book bans: prisons," *The Guardian*, September 27, 2024, https://www.theguard-ian.com/us-news/2024/sep/27/prison-banned-books.

165 Jill Eugenios, "The next chapter in record U.S. book bans? 'Soft censor-ship,'" NBC News, September 27, 2024 https://www.nbcnews.com/ nbc-out/out-news/soft-book-bans-censorship-lgbtq-race-rcna172855.

166 Andrew Albanese, "On Appeal, Llano County Seeks Book Ban Ruling That Would Upend Public Libraries," *Publishers Weekly*, September 25, 2024, https://www.publishersweekly.com/pw/by-topic/industry-news/libraries/ article/96015-on-appeal-llano-county-seeks-book-ban-ruling-that-would-upend-public-libraries.html.

167 "Zombie Comstock Law Threatens Abortion ... and Much More," Planned Parenthood, April 11, 2024, https://www.plannedparenthoodaction.org/ blog/zombie-comstock-law-threatens-abortion-and-much-more.

168 "Mandate for Leadership: The Conservative Promise," eds. Paul Dans and Steven Groves, The Heritage Foundation, 2023, https://static.project2025. org/2025_MandateForLeadership_FULL.pdf.

169 Chris Higgins, "Iowa can now enforce book ban law after appeals court overturns injunction," *Des Moines Register*, August 9, 2024, https://www. desmoinesregister.com/story/news/education/2024/08/09/appeals-court-overturns-temporary-block-on-iowa-book-ban-law-senate-file-496/747 37983007/.

170 Andrew Albanese, "Appeals Court Delivers a Mixed Decision in Iowa Book Banning Case," *Publisher's Weekly*, August 12, 2024, https://www. publishersweekly.com/pw/by-topic/industry-news/publisher-news/arti-cle/95704-appeals-court-delivers-a-mixed-decision-in-iowa-book-banning-case.html.

171 Quoted in Laura Miller, "We Are a Relatively Easy Punching Bag," *Slate*, October 3, 2024.

172 Elizabeth A. Harris, "Removing Books from Libraries Often Takes Debate. But There's a Quieter Way," *The New York Times*, October 8, 2024, https:// www.nytimes.com/2024/10/08/books/book-ban-library-weeding.html#:~:-text=But%20there%20is%20a%20quieter,out%20in%20a%20long%20time.

173 Emily J. M. Knox, "Intellectual Freedom and Social Justice: Tensions Between Core Values in American Librarianship," *Open Information Sci-ence* 4 (2020).

174 Anh Huynh, "Background Essay on Collection Development, Evaluation, and Management for Public Libraries," *Current Studies in Librarianship Journal*, 2008.

175 Toronto Public Library, "2023 Public Service Statistics, Trends & Compar-isons,"https://torontopubliclibrary.typepad.com/board-meetings/ 2024-05-27/19-2023-public-service-statistics-trends-comparisons--com-bined.pdf.

176   Daniel A. Gross, "The Surprisingly Big Business of Library E-Books," *The New Yorker*, September 2, 2021, https://www.newyorker.com/news/annals-of-communications/an-app-called-libby-and-the-surprisingly-big-business-of-library-e-books.

177   Adi Robertson, "Internet Archive appeals loss in library ebook lawsuit," *The Verge*, September 11, 2023, https://www.theverge.com/2023/9/11/23868870/internet-archive-hachette-open-library-copyright-lawsuit-appeal.

178   Sydney Johnson, "Internet Archive's Open Library Faces Uncertain Future After Court Sides With Publishers," KQED News, September 10, 2024, https://www.kqed.org/news/12003819/internet-archives-open-library-faces-uncertain-future-after-court-sides-with-publishers.

179   "Personal info, including staff social insurance numbers, stolen in Toronto library cyberattack," CBC News, November 15, 2023, https://www.cbc.ca/news/canada/toronto/toronto-public-library-ransomware-employee-data-1.7028982.

180   Frederick Douglass, "A Plea for Free Speech in Boston" (1860), National Constitution Center.

181   "Countries," *Freedom House*, https://freedomhouse.org/countries/freedom-net/scores.

182   "The Mounting Damage of Flawed Elections and Armed Conflict," *Freedom House*, 2024, https://freedomhouse.org/report/freedom-world/2024/mounting-damage-flawed-elections-and-armed-conflict.

183   *I'm Muslim And I Might Not Be Straight: A Resource for LGBTQ+ Muslim Youth*, Advocates for Youth, https://www.advocatesforyouth.org/wp-content/uploads/2018/11/Im-Muslim-I-Might-Not-Be-Straight.pdf.

184   Sikander Hashmi, "'Anti-racist' hypocrisy targets Muslim schoolchildren for their religious beliefs," *National Post*, June 15, 2023.

185   Omar Mosleh, "Protests during Pride. Pushback Against LGBTQ Events. Inside the Fight Galvanizing some Conservative Muslims in Canada." *Toronto Star*, July 30, 2023.

186   "Navigating Differences: Clarifying Sexual and Gender Ethics in Islam," Public Statement of Islamic leaders, May 23, 2023, https://navigatingdifferences.com/clarifying-sexual-and-gender-ethics-in-islam/.

187   Omar Mosleh, "Protests during Pride. Pushback Against LGBTQ Events. Inside the Fight Galvanizing some Conservative Muslims in Canada," *Toronto Star*, July 30, 2023, https://www.thestar.com/news/canada/protests-during-pride-pushback-against-lgbtq-events-inside-the-fight-galvanizing-some-conservative-muslims-in/article_ed26419e-43b7-5b6c-b793-9e0e5209ec2a.html.

188   Molly Sprayregen, "Muslim parents keep kids home in 'attendance strike' to protest LGBTQ+ books in school," *LGBTQ Nation*, October 16, 2023, https://www.lgbtqnation.com/2023/10/parents-keep-kids-home-in-attendance-strike-to-protest-lgbtq-books-in-school-citing-religion/.

189   Quoted in Tommi Laitio, "Intellectual Freedom in Toronto," Policies for Convivencia, April 3, 2024, https://tommilaitio.substack.com/p/3-intellectual-freedom.

190   Caitlyn Gowriluk, "Southern Manitoba libraries battle defunding attempts over sex-ed content in children's books," CBC News, May 1, 2023, https://www.cbc.ca/news/canada/manitoba/manitoba-library-challenges-1.6826643.

191   Author interview, September 19, 2024.

IRA WELLS is a critic, essayist, and an associate professor at Victoria College in the University of Toronto, where he teaches in the Northrop Frye stream in literature and the humanities in the Vic One program. His writing has appeared in *The Atlantic*, *Globe and Mail*, *Guardian*, *The New Republic*, and many other venues. His most recent book is *Norman Jewison: A Director's Life*. He lives in Toronto with his wife and children.